From the most successfu

secret to coaching succe

business managers and co   ..u their

teams to greatness, and exp   .vnat it takes to

build and sustain championsh.   ..ns.

Written as a series of crisp and accessible essays, *If Better is Possible* offers guidance on making important and life-changing choices, creating a culture of success, gaining mental toughness, using systems and processes to achieve a winning advantage, providing leadership opportunities, and matching competitor's ideas. It presents valuable insights into the strategic thinking behind shaping and leading an elite team.

The Author

JOHN BUCHANAN was the coach of the most successful Australian team — perhaps the most successful team ever in the history of international cricket.

During his eight years with the Australian Cricket Team, it maintained an unprecedented win ratio of seventy-five per cent or better in both Tests and One-Day Internationals. It won a record sixteen consecutive Test matches across six series and four countries, and successfully retained the Ashes. No other team in cricket history has been able to reach or sustain such a winning percentage over the same length of time: such was the success and focus of the team under Buchanan.

John has a degree in human movement, a teaching diploma and a Master of Arts in sports administration from Alberta University in Canada. He was the first cricket coach to use computer analysis of every ball bowled and has adapted his ideas on movement and motivation from a wide range of other disciplines.

IF BETTER IS POSSIBLE

JOHN BUCHANAN

Orient Paperbacks

DELHI | MUMBAI | HYDERABAD

www.orientpaperbacks.com

ISBN 13: 978-81-222-0463-6
ISBN 10: 81-222-0463-5

1st Published 2008
3rd Printing 2008

If Better is Possible

Published in arrangement with
Hardie Grant Publishing, Australia

Cover Photo by Newspix

Published by
Orient Paperbacks
(A division of Vision Books Pvt. Ltd.)
5A/8, Ansari Road, New Delhi-110 002)

Printed in India at
Ravindra Printing Press, Delhi-110 006

To my parents, who gave me my foundations, and to my wife Judith and my children Michael, Lauren, Tim, Nicholas and Elise, who have given me the backing, courage and inspiration to build on those foundations. Without their love, support and sacrifices, I would never have been able to experience such an incredible life journey.

Acknowledgements

Family is an extremely important part of my life, so I would like to acknowledge the other families that have made this book possible: my extended family, especially Pat and Barney and Judith's six brothers and sisters, the brothers and sisters I never had growing up; the cricket family, particularly the members of the Australian Cricket Team; my family of friends and supporters, who never missed an opportunity to be there when needed; and the Hardie Grant family, especially Pam: an unbelievably good team to work with.

Contents

Introduction

I HAVE DECIDED TO keep this book as simple as possible. I want you, the reader, to be able to pick it up at any time, spend twenty minutes reading a chapter of interest (or thirty minutes if you read as quickly as I do), and find messages and information that challenge you, that you recognise as common sense and that you find reassuring.

Because we are all so busy meeting the needs that each of our lives presents, I didn't want to write something that needed a reference point from the last time you were reading it. Instead, I wanted a book where you could find another chapter that appeals to you and just dive in.

Each chapter is derived from the many experiences I have been so privileged to be a part of during my eight-year stint as head coach of the Australian Cricket Team.

I haven't written it as cricket book for the sports fans. However, there are insights into this wonderful cricket team and the people who make up the side that sports fans should certainly enjoy. My purpose is to provide, through the various stories and events, a guide to navigating that busy life — be it at work, at home, in sport, or just being part of this amazing human race.

As such it is not a how-to book because, unless you are solving a mathematical problem or following one of your favourite recipes for baking a cake, I believe there are many ways to achieve the same end. And with a dash of experience and a tincture of courage, maths problems and recipes can also be attacked differently with similar success.

Therefore, I hope the book adds to, complements, or simply agrees with the navigational tools needed to deal with your daily life — no matter where you are.

I have used the sporting background of the Australian Cricket Team because that has been my life and that of my family for the best part of eight years. But more important than this, sport provides a wonderful compression of time. That is to say, sport measures teams and individuals every weekend — firstly by results good, bad or indifferent. However, a closer look at this sequence of events reveals that individuals and the teams embark on a process of readying themselves for a contest; then they compete and receive a performance measure by the completion of the game; and finally they reflect upon their success or lack of it before embarking on the same process again for the following weekend.

Such a process is what we all face in our daily lives, albeit not as visibly measured sometimes as it is in sport, but nonetheless measured, if only by our own internal recriminations or celebrations.

And so it is with one of the most successful teams the sporting world has seen. The team and the individual members within this team are faced with similar highs and lows that each of us face, even if it is in the rarefied atmosphere of international cricket. What can we learn from their travails that could be helpful to us?

Like all books and papers that we read or programs we watch and listen to, the author or authors have developed their work with a personal bias. And I must say the sentiments expressed here will be no different. Hence I think a little bit of my background will possibly assist with an understanding of why I do what I do, and why I think what I think.

I grew up on the Gold Coast when it was far enough away from the capital Brisbane to be regarded as part of country Queensland. A single child to parents Arthur and Nell, I was a late arrival and must have just sneaked in before maternal hormonal changes meant that the Buchanans were to be a childless couple.

As a consequence, I was indulged and grew up not wanting for anything. Even though my parents were from a very working class background, they were 'battlers' and determined to secure a better life for our family. I attended The Southport School, a private boys school on the Coast, where I was given a very good education and particularly enjoyed the sporting program on offer.

To compensate for the lack of siblings that I'm sure my parents wish I'd had, four of my closest friends from school, all boarders, were welcomed home on Sundays and the occasional weekend. The result was that Mal Broomhead (former CEO of Orica), Duncan Ferrier, Mark Leslie, Stu McKidd and I played endless cricket test matches in the backyard — all of us aspiring to wear the 'baggy green' cap one day. When winter rolled around, we threw in the odd rugby encounter, but we always left time for a quick cricket match before the boys had to be showered and returned to school!

University, Kings College and cricket for the University of Queensland beckoned, as it was here that the boys mentioned above had ventured a year before I was to leave the safety of home and Year 12.

Mixing with the gentlemen of Kings, as well as with the formidable numbers of university students and my heroes of University Cricket Club — Tom Veivers, Bill Buckle, Bob Crane, Dave Ogilvie, Barry Fisher, Dave Ellis, Dave Little, Charlie Mengel, Lou Cooper and Scott Ledger — soon meant my real education was well and truly under way. Somewhere along the line I managed to move from studies in Engineering to complete a degree in Human Movement Studies — a degree that revolved around sport, the study of all aspects of physical activity and movement, and a liberal spicing of very athletic young women.

At this point my cricket was going well. Having established myself on the Brisbane Grade scene then meant only one thing for a young single male — head to the UK for cricket, work, and life experience.

I trod this path for the next couple of years and was fortunate enough to be selected for Queensland to play a season of Sheffield Shield cricket in 1978–79. The experience was painful, as it promised so much, but delivered below my expectations. It ran true to my goals of playing for my uni, then Queensland, and finally, to don that 'baggy green' for Australia. But a wise person once told me, 'Son, never mix ambition with ability,' which is what I learnt through that season. My cricket dreams were shattered, but my life dreams of finding a beautiful person to spend the rest of my life with had been realised. Through a blind date arranged by one of my close mates at uni, Dr Brent Masters, I was introduced to Judith and we have been inseparable since that first night — even though she was convinced my name was Bob and I was equally convinced that I needed copious alcohol to entertain and charm this gorgeous girl.

I very much believe that every cloud has a silver lining if we are prepared to look for it in everything we do. No matter how dark the world seems there is a message for us to retrieve. And the message provides us the light and the inspiration to begin the next chapter of our journey.

The working journey thus far has taken Judith and I to Townsville, Maryborough, Edmonton (Canada), Canberra and finally back to Brisbane — and me via England, the West Indies, South Africa, India, Pakistan and Sri Lanka as well. It has brought us five absolutely great children who are each now carving out their own destinations. It has given us a wealth of personal, work and family experiences that are irreplaceable.

But most of all, each highway, each detour, each crash, each 'start again' project taught me more about myself, what I valued in life and people, and to never stop dreaming.

As you read this book, I hope my bias is not too skewed.

I also hope you enjoy and gain something from it.

1

The vision is Everest

IT IS MY VIEW that leaders, managers and coaches need to 'take people where they have never been before' as Henry Kissinger was once quoted as saying.

The role of a coach is to challenge individuals and teams with *possibilities* and take them outside their comfort zones into the realms of uncertainty. In experiencing these situations we learn more about ourselves and grow as people.

This is how a baby learns to crawl, and then walk. This is how we first learn to ride a bike. It is how we move through our education. And it is how we make it through to day two of our first job. In order to achieve milestones such as these, we are prepared to move outside the safe and comfortable 'world we know' into a world that is unknown. We usually fall down a few times, but if we get up one more time than we fall, we have learnt something new. If we don't, we won't gain that extra learning, but do discover something valuable about ourselves.

Like parenting, coaching is about creating a vision and providing a safe environment that allows individuals to fall down a number of times during their learning, their growth and their development, as they journey towards becoming a whole person.

Before I was appointed coach of the Australian Cricket Team in October 1999, I was always struck by the huge potential of the team and the players in it. I also believed the team was only scratching the surface of its potential. So, in my first meeting with the players in Brisbane before the First Test against Pakistan, I talked about a vision I saw for the team. The vision was about taking a journey together to a symbolic place called Everest. However, *Everest* is never reached because it is constantly being redefined. What we set out to achieve was a higher base camp than we had reached before.

For the first meeting I wanted to give the vision some substance. I also wanted to link history with the present, so I used the word 'invincibles'. This was the name given to the Australian cricket team captained by Sir Donald Bradman in 1948. The team journeyed to England, won the Ashes, and left the country undefeated in all their games — a feat never repeated. The vision was not that the current team be regarded as invincible, or even compared with that 1948 team. The vision for this team was to aspire to being better than it already was, and it had that capacity. Time and history will ultimately label this team and its era; however, the players had the collective abilities to take this team from being regarded as very good to one that could be referred to as great!

Steve Waugh had just taken over as captain and, while he was uncertain about the concept of 'invincible', he too shared a vision of the team putting its mark in the annals of Australian and world sporting history. Indeed, it would do this sooner than we both had envisaged. After winning the First Test against Pakistan reasonably comfortably, we miraculously won the Second Test in Hobart with a come-from-behind win — Adam Gilchrist and Justin Langer's partnership sealing one of the greatest winning chases in the fourth innings of a game.

While there is nothing like winning, there is nothing like winning the seemingly unwinnable to fuel the belief of a team. This Australian Cricket Team went on to win sixteen consecutive Test matches across six series and four countries — a record that still stands.

Having a clear vision of where you want to take people is one of the most important roles of managing and coaching a team. Everything else follows: the leadership, the team ethos and culture, the methodology for achieving the vision, and the type of people needed to drive it.

As with any team or organisation, for a vision to become reality it has to be shared by the majority of its members, especially the leaders. This can be a difficult process as different people may have a different picture of what can and should be achieved. The important role here for the coach or the leader is to recognise who the key players are and what they see as the future of the team or organisation.

I have often used various quotes from visionaries such as Sun Tzu, author of *The Art of War*, and his military principles of war to reinforce the concept behind a team's vision. A few examples of quotes that can emphasise the message behind a vision are:

- '... we are what we repeatedly do. Excellence then is not an act, but a habit ...' Aristotle.
- 'Every job is a self-portrait of the person who did it ... autograph your work with excellence ...' author unknown.
- 'If better is possible, good is not enough!' author unknown.
- 'It is not how good you are, it is how good you can be.' A former coach's comment on tennis player Roger Federer.
- 'I do not skate to where the puck is, I skate to where the puck will be." Wayne Gretsky, one of the greatest North American ice hockey players.

Spend time influencing the team visionaries to accept a common vision that then becomes part of everything done. This influencing process will take many guises and require a great deal of patience. It will not always be direct and quick. It will require placing notes under the door, circulating information, sending messages, having meetings and encouraging team members. It will require a great deal of repetition. It will also require being prepared to detour from one's direction and shelving the vision temporarily while immediate tasks and emergencies are dealt with. However, you must never lose sight of the endpoint.

Here are a few examples of the quotes I used to encourage and inspire the vision for the Australian Cricket Team:

- Aim to have history record this team and this era of Australian cricket as one of the great periods of world cricket.

- Become a great side, not just a very good side.

- Take the game to a new level by changing the way the game is played.

- Have all sides in awe of the Australian Cricket team (for the 2003 World Cup).

- Be the best skilled team the world has ever seen (for the 2007 World Cup).

- Be the first team to score 400 in One-Day International cricket.

- Be the first team to have truly multi-dimensional players (i.e. can use both sides of their body).

The vision must be inspiring to the team. It must be extremely challenging so it becomes a real test of the team's abilities. It must be exciting due to the possibility of achieving something that has not been done before. And quite probably, the vision may seem too big, too difficult, but nonetheless, it may also seem within reach.

The leader or coach must constantly monitor the progress of the vision, accelerating the climb to Everest whenever possible. If the climb has become too difficult, the coach must be prepared to ease the ascent to a 'base camp', until the time is right to begin the climb again.

KEY MESSAGES

1. The leader or coach must have a clear vision for the team or organisation.

2. The vision must be inspiring, exciting and extremely challenging.

3. The vision is designed to take the team outside its comfort zone.

4. In order to achieve a vision, it must be shared and owned by team leaders.

5. Invest time in influencing team leaders to agree on a common vision.

6. The role of the coach or leader is to constantly monitor the journey towards the vision.

2

A culture of success

WHAT HAS MADE THE Australian cricket team such a successful outfit over a long period of time? The team has been able to maintain an unprecedented win ratio of 75 per cent or better in both Tests and One-Day Internationals for more than seven years. If the numbers were to include the games that were drawn or not completed, then this result rises close to 80 per cent!

An obvious conclusion is that the team has had a group of players that are extremely talented, and there is no doubt talent plays a significant part in winning games. However, history suggests that talent alone will not produce these results. Great Australian cricket teams of past eras, such as the Bradman era (*The Invincibles*), the Chappells-Lillee-Marsh era or the West Indies era of the late 80s, were not able to reach or sustain such a winning percentage over the same length of time.

In his book *Sacred Hoops: Spiritual Lessons of a Hardwood Warrior* Phil Jackson spoke of the incredible talent in the US basketball team Chicago Bulls when he took over as coach. Players like Michael Jordan, Scottie Pippen and Toni Kukoc formed the nucleus of a side that had more talent on its bench than most other teams, but was still under performing and not winning games it should. It was only after he had players realise that they would be more successful if they worked together — *'We over I'* — that the Bulls really became a dominant force. However, to achieve this transition from an individualistic selfish approach to one that was more selfless, he needed to change and modify the existing culture within the team.

The culture of success within the Australian Cricket Team is driven by a number of elements. Let me outline which I believe to be the primary ones.

Firstly, the culture resides within and through the team members. The team is not just made up of very good cricketers, it is made up of very good cricketers with character. Matthew Hayden was returned to the Australian team to tour India in February–March 2001 not just because he was a leading contender for the opening batting position, but because Steve Waugh believed he had the type of character needed to battle the demands of a long, tough tour, on and off the field. While Justin Langer has always come under fire for his position in the team, there is no other person that any member of the team would rather to go into battle with than Justin. The Ashes Test of 2001 at The Oval in London was just one example where his fighting character was typically exemplified.

How do we know if people have character; how do we know we've got the right person? Within our support staff we have an American fielding coach, Mike Young, plus an off-beat sports psychologist, Dr Phil Jauncey. They are different to the norm. They don't subscribe to the same thinking as most of us who've practically been born into cricket. They challenge, they disagree and they often seem to talk in a different language. But the reason why they are the right people is that they share a similar vision and value system for the team, and they have similar philosophies for coaching people. And so, while their messages may be delivered in a different form, and while their approaches are not normal for cricket, I am always very confident that we are all on the same path, even though we might be getting there a different way.

Sitting right alongside character is *attitude*. Attitude is a generic term for what is imbedded within a person, or in other words, a person's inherent nature. I believe it to be something one can acquire, but it can never be taught. It comes only to the individual if he or she desires it. Attitude can be a range of emotions born from a range of personal circumstances. Therefore it will be demonstrated in a range of different ways, from positive all the way through to negative. One of the key determinants of a person's attitude is their value system — what they really value in life, in work, in sport, in society and so on. Within the cricket team there are many important values, and at the same time each person will prioritise values differently. However, it can be said that the values the Australian Cricket Team prioritise are: recognition of the position we have been given to represent Australia, aggressive fair play and winning within the rules, hard work, honesty and sincerity, family, being Australian and achieving.

In turn then, such a value system is demonstrated in the way the team plays and is perceived. The team is never satisfied with its performances. It is always seeking to raise the bar and to constantly improve. And it has a never-say-die approach. No matter what the situation, the team always believes it will find a way to win.

Then there are the *legends*, the truly great players. Within the mix of the team, we were so fortunate to have had over the last seven or so years, the *greats* in Glenn McGrath and Shane Warne, and those verging on *greatness* such as Stephen and Mark Waugh, Adam Gilchrist, Ricky Ponting and Matthew Hayden. These players exude success. They have been there and done it and in most cases continue to do it!

Another element that plays its part in enhancing the culture of success is *tradition*. Tradition is all about legacies from the past — the handing down of events, symbols, and stories that unequivocally highlight and create vivid images of what it means to be an Australian cricketer. The team song stands tall among the tangible celebrations of how success is valued and prized by all members. It is a treasured privilege to be asked to lead the team in a rendition of *Underneath the Southern Cross.*

One of the strongest and most powerful symbols of Australian cricket is the baggy green cap presented to each Test player when he is first selected to play for Australia. I am sure over the years it has had its mystical and magical powers heralded in many ways. But on the occasion of my first Test match with the team in Brisbane, November 1999, where Adam Gilchrist and Scott

Muller made their debuts, we were able to link the past with the present when Bill Brown (as I write, the oldest living Australian Test player) presented both caps.

For traditions to be embraced and become part of the *glue* that we broadly term *culture,* the *team leaders* must play a key role in the promotion of its significance and importance to the current team. This role, principally that of the captain but also the senior players, is an important legacy they leave the team. Justin Langer is renowned for his many conversations about what he calls 'the fabric' — those intangible moments and actions which define and differentiate the Australian Cricket Team.

There is no better way to develop a culture of success than winning games. It is not only winning, but also how games are won, and when and where they are won. Tight contests, come-from-behind wins, wins against the odds, series wins away from home or at the end of a torturously long season, record wins and the big trophy wins. Winning is positively infectious — and the reverse can be said of losing. It is the spirit and tonic shared by those who are a part of its making.

Having the right systems and processes in place to support the team culture is a major assistance in the development of both the team and the individuals within it. One of the systems that certainly helps to maintain this culture of success is the *reward and recognition system.* This takes many shapes and sizes, but it generally starts from where our talent is first nurtured, which is in domestic cricket. The interstate competition is a tough breeding ground for future international players. It is still a competition which differentiates players as having long-term versus short term options, and on the whole is very effective. Hence players being selected for the Australian national teams arrive with a good understanding that they can succeed at this new level.

Other mechanisms which support the reward and recognition system are:

- The player rankings and player contracts delivered by the chairman of selectors at the completion of each season.
- The peer evaluation system which is tabulated throughout a season and culminates in the players' awards night, the Allan Border Medal.

Finally, the culture of success cannot just be relied upon to be absorbed by new players, new support staff, or remain fresh in the minds of those who have been associated with the team for seasons. For the culture of success to continue it needs *constant attention and nurturing*. Keeping a very close eye on this culture is a primary role of the coach. Identifying when and why corners are being cut, understanding what the *handbrakes* are that are preventing, or will prevent, this culture from prevailing in everything the team does is a significant key to unlocking how success continues to breed success.

The *culture of success* is an extremely powerful force that can reside within every organisation. It takes time to create, capture and continue, but is a critical investment if a team, company or organisation wants to be a world leader.

KEY MESSAGES

1. Driving a culture of success is critical to the long-term success of any organisation.

2. The culture of success is made up of many elements including the right character traits, right attitude, talented staff, traditions, leadership, winning and appropriate rewards.

3. It cannot be assumed that this culture will continue to generate itself — it must be constantly revisited.

3

Everyone's a coach

'... whether you're a teacher or a committee chairman, sales manager or a choir leader, a Little League coach or a military officer, you can improve your ability to get the best performance from people.'

Everyone's a Coach, DON SHULA AND KEN BLANCHARD

WE ARE ALL COACHES in some form or other. Some of us have the title formally attached, such as the coach of a sporting team or one of the growth occupations of the twenty-first century, life coach or personal coach. Others have a less obvious acknowledgement of their coaching role, such as teachers, managers, officers in the services, ministers of the church and parents. All of these people actively engage in the very special role of coaching. So then, what is coaching?

As you can see, I differentiate very little between coaching, teaching, parenting, educating and managing. In all these occupations there are a number of key coaching principles which are delivered from a certain perspective depending on life experiences, personality, clientele and the situation. Underlying the principles I endeavour to uphold every day as a coach are *relationships* and *continual improvement*.

Before I can coach someone effectively there must be a relationship established between us. Some relationships grow quickly due to the 'chemistry' — the ease with which I can interact with someone — and that can quickly become what I call an 'honest' relationship. Other relationships may never really develop because of a lack of chemistry. In these cases each of us lacks some commonality — background, interests, friends — that means the relationship will always be distant.

Nevertheless, a distant relationship is still a relationship. In this case it means the coach is allowed only a minimal insight into the life of the person they are coaching. The trick is to find another way into understanding the individual. Generally, this is through friends, contemporaries and, sometimes, partners so that the coach is aware of what can develop and what can destroy the existing tenuous links.

Here is the first key principle: *know the whole person.*

To be a coach one must seek to build relationships with his or her charges. To do this most effectively a coach must seek to *know the whole person*, not just the athlete, the student, the staffer or the Sunday churchgoer. You need to ask yourself, 'Who is this person? What makes them tick? What and who are important in their lives? What goals are they striving for? How can I best help them?'

Everyone is different, and as coaches we need to invest time in getting to know all our 'flock' as best we can — and as much as the individual wants to let the coach into their life. I have found that when I am most satisfied with what I am doing as a coach, I am putting in time with all those around me. I feel I am 'in touch' with my players and staff. As a consequence, I believe I am in a position to best help them should it be required. Isn't this the same as parenting? Staying 'in touch' with your children and they with you means the relationship is strong and they know you are ready, willing and able to help when required. I believe business managers today don't invest sufficient time in their greatest asset and resource — their people. We are all too busy, caught up in self-directed needs, communicating through impersonal technologies and using surrogate means to superficially deal with a world of self-made complexity.

As with any relationship, the longer it lasts the more change that occurs in the person concerned. And so the coach needs to recognise these changes and be prepared to make him or herself increasingly *redundant.*

Here is the second key principle: ***create an environment of personal growth where the coach becomes increasingly redundant.***

The coach needs to keep pulling back, no longer being the directive guide, but becoming more of a safety net, and allowing the individual/athlete/child to grow. This may mean they will fall down many times, but rather than rushing to pick them up, the coach assesses their ability to pick themselves up, get back on the bike again and continue to grow.

There is no science to this process but it does stem from the relationship the coach has with the person. Knowing the individual makes a big difference in providing the best learning environment and the best way to manage redundancy.

As you can see I have made an assumption in this relationship, and that is that the individual *wants* to grow as a person. I believe this is true of all human beings. However, for a number of reasons, mainly one's environment, childhood and adolescent experiences, the desire to be better than you were yesterday is sometimes hidden. For such individuals some specialist help may need to be added to their support network.

Similarly, every coach should want his/her athlete to improve and grow. It doesn't matter what level the athlete is at, once the athlete, coach or both decide there is no room for getting better, it is time to hang the boots up and retire.

Here is the third principle: *never be satisfied.*

Never be satisfied with where we are today, because it can be better tomorrow. Shane Warne, Glenn McGrath, Adam Gilchrist, Ricky Ponting and all the greats in their respective fields follow this mantra. And these greats, whether they're in literature, ballet, sport, music or politics are only accorded such status because of their longevity and their ability to produce consistently highly skilled performances. There is little doubt that their individual skills are at the peak of their respective fields, but what has kept them there is their desire to continue to be the best — an ongoing process of not being satisfied with where they were yesterday and are today.

There are other key coaching principles such as *vision, learning, environment, culture and planning* which I will discuss in other parts of this book.

It is very important not to underestimate the role we can all play as a coach. If we see and think of ourselves as coaches, and understand that we have the capacity to influence the lives of others, both positively and negatively, then I believe we can be a very powerful force for those that we coach — whether they be families, organisations, communities or even countries!

KEY MESSAGES

1. Everyone is a coach.

2. Establish as close a relationship with your charge as that person will allow.

3. No matter how brief or distant the relationship, always try to make a difference in the life of that person.

4. Get to know the whole person.

5. Create a relationship of personal growth where the coach becomes increasingly redundant.

6. Never be satisfied with where you are today, because it can be better tomorrow.

4

Make yourself redundant

ONE OF MY MOST important roles as a coach is to make myself redundant. In fact it is the role of every parent as they help the growth of their children from the cradle to adulthood. And it should be the clear role of every manager and leader within organisations if they want the company to flourish.

What do I mean by redundancy?

Firstly, I would suggest that if you are applying for a management position within an organisation, perhaps you shouldn't mention that you seek redundancy as a management strategy. At least wait till you have a feel for the company culture before you decide to espouse the concept.

The concept of redundancy means that you are no longer needed — no longer needed to coach an individual player, players or the team. Underlying the concept of redundancy is making the player 'their best coach'.

This means that one of the principal roles of a coach is to get his/her players to know their games inside out — that is, how the individual gives him/herself the best chance of performing to their abilities. In order to achieve this result coaches must know their athletes very well. Coaches must know not only what the triggers are that allow peak performance, but also be able to read whether or not an athlete is totally in control of him/herself emotionally, so that they can initiate the triggers themselves.

A coach must be fully aware of the 'script' needed for each person to perform well. As the coach sees that an athlete knows their game inside out (i.e. they have become their best coach) and therefore in total control of their 'game', then the coach can pull back from this individual and allow them to run their own preparation and game time.

It's the same system with staff. The ideal is that the coach comes to the conclusion that everyone knows their games inside out, and so can then pull back from being intimately involved.

There are two major reasons for adopting this approach. Firstly, by withdrawing from intimate involvement with each player or staff member the coach is able to become more strategic in analysis and planning — and become more able to direct his/her energies into a range of tasks that have a long-term impact for the team, rather than just the immediate needs of each player.

Secondly, pulling back places full accountability and responsibility for performance on the individual. They learn to make consistent high-quality decisions on the field based on a detailed and well-thought-through preparation specific to their game strategy. As a coach, this is the point you want to reach with your athletes.

Of course the ideal situation rarely, if ever, arises. Players come and go from teams. Players struggle with emotional control for different reasons at different times. Staff change, which can significantly alter the team dynamics. So the coach is constantly pulling back from individuals and then returning to assist them with the learning process of their game, followed by the expansion of their game.

But while the coach constantly seeks to make the player 'their best coach', and therefore themselves redundant, the challenge is always to pull the group of individuals into a team.

This lesson was highlighted during the Australian Cricket Team's Ashes tour of England in 2005. We had a very experienced group of players, a team that was expected to continue its winning ways against the old foe. I had a new assistant coach for the tour, Jamie Siddons, who had replaced my previous assistant, Tim Nielsen. I had encouraged Tim to leave the team to broaden his coaching credentials so that when my time came to leave, he was in a much better position to apply for the job if he chose.

My coaching strategy for the tour was to pull back from the players so I could spend more time being strategic about our preparation, our opposition and about finding tasks and experiences to expand the horizons of the players. At the same time, I wanted to ensure that Jamie spent a lot of time with the players so that his relationship with each of them, and his understanding of how the team worked, were accelerated. This way, I felt Jamie would be able to replace the role that Tim had played far more quickly. With Jamie, I was going to pull back, make myself redundant — become a coaching mentor. This was to allow him to get to know the players without my interference, without having to look over his shoulder and wonder whether I would approve or not.

In hindsight, my strategy was incorrect. Jamie did get to know the players far better than he otherwise would have, and developed a strong rapport with them by the end of the trip. The players were given great autonomy as I encouraged them to work closely with Jamie and be responsible for themselves. However, the situation demanded the opposite approach. England was ready to play. They had a bowling attack which was enthusiastic, disciplined, quick and which utilised swing as a key penetrative weapon. We began the series not fully prepared for what lay ahead for a range of reasons — some in our control, some not. It was Ricky Ponting's first Ashes series as captain, which added an extra added dimension to the whole tour.

So instead of making myself redundant and creating distance between myself and the playing group, I should have made redundancy a low priority and become intimately involved with the players and all the issues they faced. I needed to be 'in the moment' with the players and not distracted by the challenging external environment.

I still, however, very much subscribe to the redundancy principle. What I learnt from the whole experience was not about compromising my principles. It was about being very aware of maintaining close contact with the total group so that I could make better decisions about the best mix of coaching principles to be employed.

KEY MESSAGES

1. Every coach's role is to make themselves redundant.

2. Making the athlete 'their best coach', allows a coach to pull back and move towards redundancy.

3. There is a constant process of being redundant, then moving back close to an athlete, then realising when it is time to pull back again.

4. When you make yourself redundant, ensure you still have good rich contact with your athletes so that danger signals to athlete or team can be quickly identified.

5. Redundancy is one of a set of principles, and its priority for implementation will always vary between low and high.

5

Another way

HOW MANY TIMES HAVE you been confronted with a problem or a task that seems impossible to solve... until someone else comes along and solves it quickly because they view it from a different perspective?

I am a great admirer of the educator and author Edward de Bono and how he challenges our conventional thinking, or at least the way we learn or are taught to think. Through such techniques as provocation, creative thinking and concept research and development — dealing in possibilities, searching for alternatives, and questioning existing ideas and paradigms — de Bono clearly demonstrates untapped human potential.

So it can be in any field of endeavour. There are many examples of potential being reached through different ways of thinking in sport, but one that stands out for me is from the book *Moneyball: The Art of Winning an Unfair Game* by Michael Lewis. In short, a baseball team called the Oakland A's was finding it difficult to compete with some other major league teams, such as the New York Yankees, due to the amount of money they could spend on contracting players at draft time. The Yankees, which had at least three times the buying ability, could effectively buy the best of the draft while the A's had to be content with lower end draftees. In essence this meant that the A's could never compete with any consistency during the season as the depth of quality on its playing list was substantially less than other teams.

The A's manager, Billy Bean, believed there had to be another way to look at the problem. So he went back to basics and asked himself: what wins a baseball game? Answer: scoring more runs than the opposition. Next question: how do you score runs? Answer: by getting players on base.

Bean used this information and looked at the statistics and, to a lesser extent, the scouting reports on all draftees, college and high school baseball players. What he found was that those players most effective at getting on base were not, in fact, the top end draft picks. Many of these players were less fashionable, less likely to enthuse the talent scouts, and therefore resided in the mid-to-lower sections of the draft.

But Bean directed his attention to these players and within a couple of years the A's were playing the Yankees for the right to go to the World Series. Since that time the A's have been consistent performers in terms of making the end-of-season play offs.

I have always felt the same way about cricket. Cricket is a statistician's utopia, with numbers and records for everything imaginable. However, many of these numbers date back to when the game began. For example, we still look at the number of 50s or 100s players make, the number of five wickets per innings or ten wickets per match, the averages of bowlers and batters, the number of catches fielders make and so on. While these numbers are factual and are a linking thread through history, are they the best numbers to be used to gain a measure on how individuals and teams perform over time?

For instance, why should 50 runs today be considered the same as 50 made in the early 1900s when there were uncovered wickets, different outfields, less protective equipment used, less sophisticated bats available, and less athletic players? Indeed, why should a 50 scored by Glenn McGrath be considered the same as 50 scored by Ricky Ponting?

If we are to better understand performance, we need to be more like Billy Bean and look at the numbers behind the numbers. In business, these numbers are often called *key performance indicators* (KPIs) and can refer to teams as well as individuals.

David Parkin, who was coach of Carlton's 1995 AFL premiership team, sought out one of these KPIs and called it 'sacrificial acts'. These were actions taken by players during a game that were done to help the team, but not represented on the normal game statistics sheet. He honed this measure to a point where he could show that if the team exceeded a certain number for the match they were never beaten. This measure is now widely used in AFL statistical analysis.

We are still in the process of mining our numbers, but I believe that overall team and individual performances are linked to such new KPIs as:

- Scoring shot percentage — the number of scoring shots made by a batter compared with the number of balls faced.

- Dot ball percentage — the number of dot balls bowled by a bowler compared with the number of balls bowled.

- Percentage of consecutive overs of three runs and under (for test cricket), five and under (for ODI cricket) — the number of three and under, and five and under, overs bowled consecutively compared with total overs bowled.

- Understanding how the KPIs above are affected by phases of play (e.g. Power Plays in ODI), or by playing at home or away, or by batting first or second, or by playing day or day–night games.

- Better measurement of our fielding through a summation of fielding error numbers, fielding effort numbers, throwing accuracy and catches (catches are sorted by three levels of difficulty: easy, difficult, rare).

Trends across certain KPIs should emerge that directly correlate to wins and losses by the Australian Cricket Team.

The consequences of these correlations will directly impact on training, coaching techniques and, ultimately, the way the game is played. This is not to say that the numbers will supersede experience, intuition and knowledge — the numbers should be a complementary tool in the development of players and teams.

It is essential that the thinking that drives current paradigms is challenged. As Edward de Bono and John Lyons wrote in their book, *Marketing Without Money: How 20 top Australian entrepreneurs crack markets with their minds,* there are a number ways this can be achieved:

- Always look for alternatives — is there another way, a better way? Challenge existing ideas and develop concepts first.

- Focus your thinking — be very clear what the aim, goal and purpose is.

- Be creative — use techniques such as *random entry* (selecting ideas at random), *concept fans* (development of ideas by exploring layer after layer) and *provocation* (interruption of current pattern by means of word, action, statement), to assist the search for alternatives.

- Finally, the reality check — this includes *harvesting* all the thinking, ideas and concepts, then *reviewing* them for what can or cannot work.

Obviously this process is ongoing. However, if an organisation embraces the process as part of its culture, then it can be more proactive to environmental change. It can understand the type of people who are important for the organisation to meet its vision. It can change the game, or at least, have significant competitive advantage over its opposition.

The capacity for any team to look at the same problem from different perspectives gives it a range of options and a range of possibilities — all necessary for any team to give itself the best chance of continued success.

KEY MESSAGES

1. Challenge conventional thinking.

2. Define your KPIs — the ones that really make a difference.

3. Compile and use statistics that help measure your KPIs.

6

John who?

IN JUNE 1994 I was selected to take over the role of coach of the Queensland Cricket Team.

This was a significant event given I had just unseated one of Queensland's and Australia's favourite sons and cricket legend, Jeff Thomson. Thommo had been doing the job for four years and had come close on at least one occasion to winning what was then known as the Sheffield Shield for Queensland.

It was a major appointment given that Queensland was still chasing its first title since entering the competition in 1926. It had, on more than one occasion, seemingly had the Shield in its grasp only to be denied by some event contrived by the gods, or as Queensland supporters would view it, the southern States. Since the early 1960s when the enigmatic Wes Hall steamed, flailed and calypsoed his way in from the Vulture Street end, Queensland had sought, through a variety of high profile international coaches and player/coaches — Tom Graveney, Vivian Richards, Majid Khan, Alvin Kallicharan, Rusi Surti,

Greg Chappell and Allan Border — to wrest the chalice from the grip of the southerners.

So when my appointment was announced, it was met with silence from some quarters and vitriol from others. Greg Ritchie for one, a long-time servant of Queensland cricket and a wearer of the baggy green himself, lambasted the choice in his role as local radio host and as his satirical character Mahatma Coat. His acerbic humour and his penchant for verbal attacks were certainly directed my way. Mind you, he was not alone, although most others who chose to make comment were somewhat more balanced in their criticism.

However, the fundamental question that kept reverberating in the corridors of Queensland cricket was ... John who?

Who was this bloke who had only played seven first class games for Queensland, and one of his main claims to fame was that he'd scored a duck on just about every ground in Australia! His cricket career had virtually been terminated at that point and now, sixteen years later, he is chosen to coach a team that has not been able to win the competition for sixty-nine years. Furthermore, he is required to coach international players of the calibre of Allan Border (who initially was playing one last year of first class cricket), Craig McDermott, Ian Healy, Carl Rackemann, Greg Rowell, Michael Kasprowicz, Matthew Hayden and Stuart Law! And the guy hasn't even played the game at this level! How could he know what it takes to play in the tough cauldron of first class cricket, let alone international cricket?

Well, the fact remains that those who raised these objections were absolutely correct to a point. I certainly had no experience of what it was like to continually do battle in the middle for state or country, and I didn't know what it was like to savour success or lack of success at this level of cricket over an extended period of time.

What I did know, though, was myself, my methodology and my vision. I also knew enough of the Queensland history and the agony the players, public and sponsors had endured. I had spoken with the Queensland captain and legendary Australian wicket keeper, Ian Healy, prior to my interview for the position and asked him hypothetically, that if I was appointed coach, whether I'd be given a reasonable shot at the job by the senior players and squad. If his answer had been negative or equivocal I would not be writing this book now. I simply would not have applied.

I believed that at forty-one years of age, I had a range of different experiences behind me that would equip me for the role. I had been a player who tried but did not succeed on the first-class cricket field; I had been a sports administrator working for the Townsville City Council, the XII Commonwealth Games and the Australian Volleyball Federation. I had been an educator who studied and worked in TAFE, travelled overseas to Canada to obtain a Masters degree and lectured in Sports Studies in Canberra. I had acted as a manager coordinating the joint Federal–State Aussie Sports program for children in Queensland, as well as other state sporting programs within the Queensland government. I was a parent of five young children — although I'd often made their life difficult with relocations around the world. I had also worked as a sport coach involved with junior and senior clubs before finally returning to the University of Queensland Cricket Club to assess my philosophy and methods with a group of players who were to be the future of Queensland cricket.

In hindsight, another intangible piece of experience was that I did not carry the weight of *historical baggage* that all those in and around Queensland cricket carried year after year. Obviously, with each passing year the weight grew heavier and heavier for those entrusted with its portage — especially the players.

In the course of my interview for the position of head coach, I clearly stated the vision for Queensland cricket under my stewardship. My vision was not to just win the State title for Queensland, but to put in place systems and processes that would allow Queensland to dominate domestic cricket for the next decade. Along the way, we would win the four-day and one-day titles, but our attention had to be shifted from result to process.

If I was to be offered the coaching job, I needed to know that everybody understood my philosophy and approach, and this would be part and parcel of the package that they were getting. It was the way I had operated in my previous jobs. It was a way that I understood and was comfortable with. It was a way I could deliver and, most importantly, I knew it worked.

What I didn't know was whether it was the way that would assist Queensland cricket in the short term — that is, to get immediate results. And my philosophy and approach certainly flew in the face of standard business practice. However, it's important to back yourself in these situations.

As a result, I took on the job armed with a range of tools and knowledge that gave me confidence in my methods, although I knew this gave me no guarantee of job security, let alone being successful in the role.

I also realised that the outcome might not go my way. I might in fact be the right person at the wrong time, or the wrong person for the time. But the important thing was to stay true to my direction regardless of results. In this case it meant putting my direction and goals ahead of hanging onto the job and getting an early win for Queensland. I had got the job on the basis of turning Queensland into a cricket power, not a weekly winner — that would follow. And I could not compromise my principles simply to save myself or to meet short-sighted gratification.

So I brought some short-, medium- and long-term planning to the team. Other elements that I added were a more precise and structured feedback and analysis system. This system was both formal and informal and included, for the first time, computer technology to aid getting specific information and analysis back to our players, as well as carrying out detailed analysis of our opposition. To be successful I had to find the right personnel. Queensland cricket — and now Australian cricket and other sports around the world — was extremely fortunate to have one of the best coaches working virtually unrecognised in their midst, Jim Hunter. And even greater fortune shone our way as Jim's brother, Richard, was a computer programming genius. Together we developed a technology system that no-one else had or had even dreamed of. It took years to refine, and long unpaid hours of trial and error. But these days the Hunter brothers' company FairPlay is a market leader in the provision of technology support to national and international sporting teams.

I changed our training systems to make them inclusive rather than exclusive — the young and the old, the first-time squad member and the Australian representative working together in the gym and on the training field. There were no exclusions, and each learnt from the other, be it in training, in competition or in social settings.

We improved our preparation for games with review and preview meetings, with game footage to highlight what we did well, what wasn't working as well, and identify the patterns of play that we could expect from our opposition.

Regardless of these changes, we had definite periods in that first season and, in fact, throughout the time I was coaching Queensland, where results were craved. But it was a case of sticking to what I believed in: keeping the team's attention on the process and letting the results look after themselves. It was a case of believing in myself and backing my approach, even though the doomsayers and doubters were never very far away.

Through the first season we had some outstanding wins: beating South Australia and Victoria at the Gabba in three days, an Allan Border and Carl Rackemann inspired win in Melbourne, as well as some thrashings by New South Wales and South Australia away, and the odd draw.

Making the Shield final came down to the last game. There were four teams in contention: Victoria, Western Australia, South

Australia and Queensland. After day one of the last round, South Australia was in a strong position against New South Wales, Victoria and Western Australia were playing each other, and we were on the ropes against Tasmania, having been bowled out for 234 and Tassie were 0 for 50.

The Queensland players were definitely carrying the weight of expectations on their shoulders throughout the first day. They were playing on a knife-edge, as if their very lives depended on the result — an outright win would guarantee Queensland hosting their first ever Sheffield Shield.

A famous (or at least match-turning) dressing room scene took place at the end of the first day. It was my task to wipe out any negatives which had occurred on the field and prepare them to come back ready to play in the morning.

The next three days of the game saw the Queensland team play some of their best cricket. They won the game outright, and took this momentum and confidence to the Gabba where they played South Australia in the 1995 Sheffield Shield final, which they won.

KEY MESSAGES

1. Know yourself — your philosophy, principles and methodology.

2. Have confidence in and back yourself.

3. Do not compromise who you are to secure your position or a result.

7

Life is about choices

IT WAS MY SECOND year of coaching the Queensland Sheffield Shield side and we were about to embark on a tour to Victoria, a critical match for the success or otherwise of the season.

We had some new faces in the team that year, one of them being a chap by the name of Adam Dale. He had put together some outstanding club and Second XI performances for the past couple of seasons, and had already made an impression at interstate level, principally through one-day cricket.

There were only one or two people in our team like Adam who were playing first-class cricket while holding down a full-time job and managing a family. At the time Adam was a sales manager for Nike and, I believe, a highly regarded member of the national Nike team.

Adam is an ambitious person. Not a stand-all-over-the-next-person-to-get-what-I-want ambitious; rather a person who sets himself a vision of what he wants to be, the goals that he needs to kick to get there, and then goes about achieving them.

Life is about choices

Adam had moved from Victoria with Nike to take up an opportunity to help the Brisbane office grow the brand. He had a young wife and plans for a family, he had settled into the Brisbane lifestyle but he also wanted to continue to play cricket, which was more than just a passion.

Adam knew he had ability. He set himself a vision for cricket, which was to play at the highest level he could. However, he was constantly being faced with the feedback that he was not quick enough as a pace bowler to succeed at first-class cricket. Well, for an ambitious person such statements were only further incentives to achieve his dream of playing cricket for Australia.

When Adam was picked for our Sheffield Shield team to travel to Victoria he was over the moon! He was kicking the goals that he believed one day would see him play for Australia. But there was one major obstacle to him achieving his sporting ambition — commitment!

A couple of days before we were due to leave as a team to Melbourne, Adam came to me and said that there was a major conference with his employer Nike that he needed to attend. The conference overlapped our travel to Victoria and so he would not be able to travel with the team, but would be able to meet us the following day and have time to prepare with us then.

Adam knew that I encouraged all our players to have balance in their lives and not place all their eggs in one basket. In this way the highs and lows that cricket (or indeed sport) delivers are not massively magnified by the individual's life revolving solely around their success or otherwise on the cricket field. So

I imagine Adam expected a very sympathetic and empathetic hearing, one that would allow him to achieve both the conference and the preparation with the team.

If this same situation had arisen in years earlier when cricket was still a game, a game played hard on the field, it would have been okay. In those days little attention was paid to the meticulous preparation that is needed for individuals and a team to properly ready themselves for competition in today's world of sport. But I was part of the new broom approach — sweeping some of the old habits away. One of these was definitely about the concept of 'team'. For me, 'team' means we are all in it together. No one is bigger than the group. We share the celebrations as well as the commiserations. We understand the sacrifices that are required to be successful and we never stop trying to find ways to improve.

So my answer to Adam's request was 'no'. It was qualified though. If he wanted to be a regular and valuable member of this team, he had to make a clear choice between cricket and work. If he chose the conference (and I had no problem with him making that choice, except for the fact that we would lose a very good player), then there was no room for him in our team. I believed it was extremely important for his career, cricket, and for his future family life, that he was forced to make a decision which would commit him to giving himself the best chance of chasing his ambitions and dreams.

It was an interesting couple of hours as Adam struggled to initially understand why I would say no and I kept harping away that 'life was all about choices'.

Life is about choices

In making a choice, one needs to accept there will be consequences. Adam's choice was to try to have the best of both worlds. The consequence of that choice was that he would be excluded from the Queensland cricket team's way of doing things. Adam needed to examine his choice so that he was happy and would continue to be happy with the outcomes. If he was, then he was committing to his work career and placing cricket as a lower priority. The team would respect Adam's choice whichever he chose.

Fortunately for Queensland and Australian cricket, Adam chose to come with us to Melbourne. He went on to be one of Queensland's finest bowlers and was chosen to play for Australia on several occasions. He now has retired from first-class cricket; he has returned to the workforce as a very successful executive and has a beautiful young family. Adam and I remain close friends and often joke about that day and how everything we do in life is about choices.

Often we make choices to avoid conflict; we take the easy road and do nothing at all rather than the road less travelled and stand up for what we believe in. Whatever choice we make, we need to understand there are always consequences of that choice. And we are the ones that made it, no one else. We are accountable.

I often hear myself saying, 'I wish I had not done it that way' or 'If only I had thought about it first' or 'I wonder what would have happened if I had chosen that path over the one I took?' But the reality is, I made the decision, good or bad. It can't be changed after the event. But hopefully, I would learn from it, and if I didn't, then I missed an opportunity by making a poor choice. We should not regret the life choices we make, the choices we make every day. It is how we learn more about ourselves and, like Adam Dale, it allows us to keep chasing our dreams.

KEY MESSAGES

1. Be clear on what your goals and ambitions are.

2. Clarity on what dreams you are chasing will allow for better choices and decision-making.

3. Making a choice to chase something drives commitment.

4. All choices have consequences — be prepared to accept them without regret.

5. All choices provide the opportunity to learn more about ourselves.

8

What is a team?

ON 29 JULY 2007, the Australian cyclist Cadel Evans achieved a significant milestone in Australian history (and in my opinion not just sporting history) by coming second in the Tour de France. He is the first Australian to have stood on the podium at the conclusion of the world's most famous cycling race — a race that seduces television audiences around the world.

Le Tour is an event that demands incredible endurance, tactical, mechanical and team skills from each and every rider. The 2007 race comprised twenty stages over twenty-two days, was some 3,550 kilometres in length, and began in London, traversed Belgium and France, and finished on the Champs-Élysées, Paris. The Spaniard Alberto Contado won in ninety-two hours and twenty-six seconds with Cadel Evans just twenty-three seconds from claiming the coveted yellow jersey — twenty-three seconds over 3,550 kilometres! Evans lamented that his team of support riders was unable to work for him during one of the last climbing stages through the Pyrenees and he lost a frustrating fifty-five seconds to the eventual winner.

Sports such as cycling, golf, swimming, downhill skiing, tennis, karate, motor sports and so on are regarded as individual sports. Success is regarded as an individual effort rather than a team one. Clearly, Cadel Evans' comments indicate something else — that is, what *individual sport* is all about… teams. It is the hidden figures in the background, those whom the searchlight never sees, who comprise the *team* behind the athlete — the support riders, coaches, mechanics, medical personnel, managers, statisticians and the public relations group, etc.

When I'm asked about cricket, my view is that it is also an individual sport… an individual sport dressed up in team clothing. Like the sports mentioned above, once on the playing field a cricketer is on his/her own. There is only one ball to hit, bowl or field, and only one person to do it. Cricketers can't rely on anyone else to make a decision for them, they can't rely on a team-mate placing the ball in the right position to hit, or restricting an opposition batter so that a bowler can take a wicket.

However, for a player to be best prepared for on-field performance it takes a huge off-field support team, with the addition of team-mates who are extensively involved in training and preparations, to enable them to achieve the desired results. I don't have any doubt that outstanding individual performances are due to a total and concerted team effort.

What type of team helps create the best on-field performance and how is it done? Let's start with the key qualities of a top high-performance team:

- Clarity of vision which is shared by the team members.

- Strong leadership.
- Very skilful athletes and a depth of talent.
- Strong value systems that place priority on mateship, family, hard work, continual improvement, integrity, honesty, innovation, courage, humility, fun and enjoyment, fairness and loyalty.
- A culture of success comprised of rich traditions and symbols; risk taking and backing your skills; learning and personal growth; accountability and responsibility; never being satisfied with performance; a never-say-die approach to any situation; respect for self, others and the game.
- A system that practises detailed planning, preparation and benchmarking; places process first and result second; values partnerships (teams within teams); balances playing in the moment while seeking to control the future; produces quality athletes; utilises a full leadership approach.
- The team is surrounded and supported by the right people.

Most analysts would agree that these are the ingredients of a high performance team. So how does one measure whether the 'team' is up to the standards of expectation? There is the obvious measure, a clear demonstration of high performance both by the team and individuals within the team.

In addition, there are other less visible measures:

- Team members will defend and protect each other from what they see as attacks from outside the team.
- The team will develop its own self-regulatory system with its own standards that are enforced by key members.

- The team treasures its uniqueness and allows entry only through association and introduction by a team member.
- The intangible strength of a team will be determined by the degree to which it holds to these measures.

And there are two other even more subtle measures that go to the very essence of 'team' — *selflessness* and *discretionary effort*.

Each member of the team has a job to do, and there is a high expectation by themselves and by other team members that they will perform their job to those expectations. In order to perform consistently to and beyond expectations, each team member needs to clearly know what they require and ensure (or demand if necessary) that their needs are provided for. For this reason they are often very self-centred, selfish individuals, but that is precisely what they need to be to survive at a high performance level.

However, to be part of a high-performance team each individual recognises that every other team member is in exactly the same position. As a consequence, team members work out ways in which their personal needs are met while at the same time the needs of other team members are also being satisfied.

Selflessness requires compromise by both individuals and groups of individuals in:

- Training sessions.
- The amount of time an individual would prefer to devote to an activity.
- Doing things that are not relevant to personal needs.
- Planning well ahead to ensure they get their specific needs.

The experienced athlete knows that their turn will come for their specific demands. In the meantime, some personal sacrifice for a team-mate's cause will take priority.

Discretionary effort is the combined outcome of team members knowing what has to be done, having the self motivation to do it and acknowledging that while there will be potential personal gain, the team will also benefit. This is often described as 'going that extra bit' or 'doing the hard yards' or 'doing their bit for the team'. Unless there is a *team* environment this extra effort occurs inconsistently, or only in certain individuals who stand out.

KEY MESSAGES

Rather than specific messages this time, answer the following questions with respect to your notion of *team*. Then you can understand what needs to be addressed in order to improve. There are many more questions that can be asked, but the honest answers to these should provide a good starting point for developing a high-performance team.

1. What is your view of an ideal high-performance team — in regards to people, culture, actions and behaviours?

2. Rate where your team sits on a scale of 1 to 10 with 10 being the top.

3. If there is a gap between your rating and 10, what are the obstacles (the handbrakes) preventing the team being a 10?

4. Would your players view it differently? If so, what would they rate the team, and what would they see as obstacles or handbrakes?

5. If there are differences, what's causing the 'gap' and why do you think this is the case?

9

Role models

ONE OF THE BY-PRODUCTS of our modern society appears to be an increasing emphasis placed upon people who have been accorded the status of 'role model'. While role models can come from any strata of society, they are generally people with a high profile who are perceived to exert an influence on younger people through their actions and words. Common role models include church leaders, political leaders, business leaders, community leaders and sportsmen and women.

The adulation and acclaim of role models in society is not a new phenomenon. We know from our history books that all sorts of people have been perceived as role models, from Jesus Christ right through to the 'crocodile hunter', Steve Irwin.

Society expects its role models to be pillars of virtue, ethically and morally unquestionable, with exemplary work and social habits. We want them to inspire us to be more like them.

Sportsmen and women in particular are viewed by many parents as being role models in the development of their children. As I watch members of our Australian cricket team be swamped by enthusiastic supporters — children and adults alike — all seeking a piece of their heroes, I see young men who have exceptional physical and mental skills being required every moment of the day and night to possess the same level of emotional, social and spiritual skills.

Our team members range in age from twenty-one to thirty-seven. While all have at least either made it to Year 12 or completed their formal school education, and some have even gone onto further education, the workforce, or have young families to care for, their lives have, for the most part, been defined by and sacrificed for the pursuit of one aim — to play cricket for Australia.

While it can be said that these players travel the world, meet incredible people and have experiences that most of us can only dream of, the playing, training and the preparing for cricket is still central to everything they do. These young men, whom society accords as role models, end up having a very insular upbringing and somewhat narrow ongoing life education.

Many of these players have sacrificed a tertiary education, been unable to experience a typical youth to early adulthood development and have lived in a world that is atypical — a world that is, or can become, a fantasy land. Often these young men have been protected or shielded by parents, coaches, older siblings and friends from the responsibilities and accountabilities that community and society demand of everyone else.

As a consequence, a significant percentage will often lack appropriate vocabulary, diction and grammar. They will be ignorant of some behaviours deemed appropriate (or inappropriate) by society, such as common courtesy, and they can develop an arrogant attitude through being sheltered by their minders from accepting normal punishments and censure. It is almost inevitable that they will fall short of being the statesman-like person that is expected of a role model.

The bottom line is that *most* talented sports people have never asked to be role models. They do not have the skills, the personal background or the intention of fulfilling the role that society has prescribed for them. In fact, it is almost a rite of passage that if a person, in sport or otherwise, is everything we want them to be, society will want to cut them down, to find something wrong with them, to bring the so-called tall poppy back to the field.

In that respect, community and society have a lot to answer for. We abrogate our responsibilities by making the world a less environmentally safe and healthy place to live, we place individual and material needs above a sense of community and cooperation, and we provide less and less moral direction for our children with the gradual breakdown of the extended family and the family unit. In their place we position our adulation of sporting role models as a surrogate solution for what should be the responsibilities of the adult population.

Each of our players confronts, or is faced with, these issues associated with being perceived as a role model in different ways. For instance, Damien Martyn is a person who prefers to be less visible socially than other players. However, being a senior player, who played both Test and One-Day Cricket, he was unable to remain secluded from the glare of public scrutiny and appreciation. While his performances and that of the team met the continued high expectations, Damien's low-key approach to being a high-profile role model survived. When expectations were incongruent with performance, then Damien's attributes as a person, his rights to be selected as a player and his behaviours as a role model to all fans and aspiring cricketers were constantly questioned, due to his personal preference for a low profile.

On the other hand, Adam Gilchrist is more accessible to the public, media and corporate sector. Consequently, Adam is perceived to be an outstanding role model due to his on-field successes, his natural abilities to engage the media and his outstanding personal character, which is clearly visible for all to see.

The personal choices made by each individual on how accessible to the media they wish to be can have significant ramifications on how they are represented.

If I mention the names Shane Warne, Stuart MacGill, Glenn McGrath, Ricky Ponting, Matthew Hayden or Justin Langer, we will immediately share different opinions as to these players' suitability to be placed in the position of role models for our children and our communities.

Our opinions of these players are firstly guided by their sporting performances — Australian sporting successes are revered in our culture! However, once a player's on-field box has been ticked, then we want them to have all the magic and goodness of Peter Pan and Tinkerbell — we want to idolise them in every possible way. When fantasy meets reality, or at least perceived reality, there is often a let-down. Our heroes are not always who we want them, wish them or will them to be. They are in fact, just like you and me — young men who have a special gift, but are forged in the frailties of the same society from which we want uplifting.

There is definitely a place for our sports role models because we naturally appreciate unique skills of our sporting heroes. But we can't expect them to be perfect. We can't expect them not to have the same warts and blemishes we all carry. And we can't expect all of them to be exactly the same — a few will be able to meet societal expectations; most will fall short at some point. But that is not their fault! It is ours, because we cannot find it in ourselves to live a role model existence and are happy to point the finger at everyone else, but ourselves.

These messages, I think, are very clear for the business world. Like sporting stars, the star performers in business receive rich accolades from their peers, staff, their company and the industry they work in. But we must be careful not to cast that successful person as a role model without flaws. While he or she may have work attributes and/or personal traits that are worth modelling, regarding them as infallible will be a dangerous precedent, as very few can meet and sustain such labelling.

Role models, or behaviours and character that should be modelled, are not always found in the high achievers — far from it. People who conduct themselves totally professionally at work no matter what the level or occupation, or those who live their personal lives according to the principles of fairness, honesty, respect for all and so on are very important role models for our busy daily lives.

Role models

For those in leadership roles, such as board members, CEOs, directors or school principals, there is a requirement to *walk the talk*. The people who occupy such roles are the organisation's 'parents'. As a consequence, they cannot escape their responsibilities of demonstrating the appropriate work behaviours and attitudes that are part of the organisation's culture. They cannot defer to an organisational hero or star to be the role model for their staff members. Sure, there will be outstanding organisational performers whose standards can be highlighted and applauded, but just as parents are found wanting by allowing outside role models to be the guiding lights for their children, so too will organisational leaders. Whatever behaviours and actions are championed and valued by the organisation, the captain of the team must lead by example.

KEY MESSAGES

1. Do not expect the stars of our community to display all the values, behaviours and attitudes that we would like to have, but are unable to live by ourselves.

2. Understand which values, behaviours and attitudes are important to your organisation and champion those through the deeds of a range of people within the team or company.

3. Be aware that not all people want to be accorded role-model status.

4. The formal leadership team of the organisation must not only espouse the values, behaviours and attitudes that are critical to it, but must live them.

10

Expectations

ON WEEKEND MY WIFE and I were fortunate enough to be invited to watch a couple of our favourite football teams do battle. On the Saturday night we saw the Australian Rugby Union team (the Wallabies) play New Zealand (the All Blacks), in the second game in the Bledisloe Cup series. On the Sunday we saw Rugby League team the Brisbane Broncos play the Wests Tigers — it was just a few rounds before the National Rugby League finals series.

Now, as a footballer I am a pretty good cricketer, so I try not to be too analytical about the way teams and individuals play. I simply try to enjoy the spectacle, although I must admit to carrying sufficient bias to feel aggrieved by certain refereeing calls which did not favour the Wallabies or the Broncos.

Being a guest of the ARU and Broncos management means we are seated with the various officials, friends and families of each organisation. In doing so we spend time in conversation and share in the emotions of the occasion.

Both games finished with similar results. The All Blacks prevailed to win the Test thirteen points to nine while the Broncos went down twenty to six. Coming into the match, the Wallabies had had a resounding win over South Africa the week before, but had been outclassed two weeks previously by the All Blacks. The Broncos had lost their last two games which moved them from top of the table to third position.

Both teams have a proud history. The feats of both teams, and the individuals within those teams, are legendary. And their respective trophy cabinets overflow with the booty of past glories.

On this weekend though, the *expectations* for each of those teams were different. Yes, every true Australian rugby supporter wanted Australia to win, but realised they were playing a side that, at that point in time, appeared to have too much class. As spectators, we expected Australia to put up a good showing and a much improved result on their last game against the All Blacks … but a win? Well, that seemed against the odds.

On the other hand the Broncos had the home-ground advantage. According to all the experts, they had played poorly the previous week against the superior North Queensland Cowboys. However, this week they were playing a team much lower on the premiership table and were expected to win. In fact, in some of the pre-game conversation, club officials said that they were more concerned about the tough games ahead leading to the finals than the current game!

As I said, both teams lost. However, the Wallabies went close to achieving over what was expected, so the mood in the camp was relatively buoyant, given that had just lost the Bledisloe Cup!

The atmosphere in the Broncos camp was totally different. The mood was sombre, heads were shaking, and people were asking: 'Who's to blame? How could they lose to the Tigers? At home?' The players and coach were not sure where to turn next — they were even looking at next season already!

Well, I am not a football coach, but I am a coach. And I have been surrounded and engulfed by *expectations* many times before with the Australian and Queensland cricket teams.

Firstly, let's understand what expectations are so that then we can begin to deal with them.

Expectations arrive in two packages: external and internal.

External expectations are driven by the media, history, friends, marketing, previous results and organisations. These expectations are *outside* the control of the team or the athlete but fuel the hype that exists around the contest. The 2006–07 Ashes series in Australia is the perfect example of how external expectations, such as the ones above, combined to fuel not only an expectation of how good the series would be, but also how well Australia would do throughout it.

External expectations are inescapable. They are embedded in every conversation and are thrust in your face from every section of the media from the moment the radio or TV goes on. They travel to the breakfast room; to the pre-game and in-game interviews and commentary. It is part of the environment in which the Australian Cricket Team (and any high-profile athlete or celebrity) lives. The greater the stakes are perceived to be, the greater the level of expectation on the team to deliver.

Expectations

The other type of expectation is internal. This is the one that is derived from the players themselves, which in turn is derived from those around them, as well as their past achievements. In the case of this particular cricket team, some of its members, such as Glenn McGrath and Shane Warne, have been on the international sporting stage for a dozen years or more, while the majority of the others have also played internationally for a decade.

The majority of the team has also been associated with some historic wins, such as the come-from-behind victory against Pakistan, in the Second Test in Hobart of the 1999–2000 series. Other achievements include the world record sixteen consecutive Test victories, fourteen consecutive One-Day International wins, a world record at the time, domination of most teams who visited Australia between 1999 and 2007, three World Cup wins in a row, stunning individual performances by the opening partnership of Matthew Hayden and Justin Langer, Ricky Ponting and Hayden being accorded the world's number one batsmen, the wicket-keeping and batting feats of Adam Gilchrist, the world-record wicket takers in McGrath and Warne, the thunderbolts propelled by the blond bombshell Brett Lee, and the hitting feats and charisma of Andrew Symonds. The list goes on.

So as the players assemble for a Test match, a One-Day International, a tour or simply a training session, they arrive with a background of outstanding performances. They have an inner confidence, an inner arrogance and a self-belief that their skills and their combined talents are superior to the opposition. Even if an individual is down on personal performance, he is able to drink from the success of the others which whisks away any fears and uncertainties. It is a dressing room of champions, of battle-hardened warriors, who all have the desire to engage and defeat the next opposition.

Consequently, each individual within the team carries this *internal expectation* to win every time they set foot on the playing arena. There are no thoughts of second prize because that is no prize at all! So how does the team deal with this constant level of expectation?

For most of the time, I think the team manages internal and external expectations very well. At the conclusion of a winning game, it is important to understand that only two or three players may have played to their expectation. Another four or five players may have played below their expectations, but met the expectations of those external to the team. This leaves three or four players who did not impact on the game by any measure of expectations.

And herein lies the means to deal with and manage expectations. It is about diverting the emotions of expectations into the reality of those things we can measure and those things we can control.

We had a few regular mantras we used within the team:

- Play on skill, not emotion.
- Control the controllables.
- Play in the moment.

Expectations

These simple phrases often help to remind us as a team that if we allow ourselves to get caught up in the emotional game of expectations, we have become distracted from the task at hand. Once distracted, we are as vulnerable as any team because we are not playing *our game!* We're playing somebody else's. As individual players and as a team we need to deal only with the present state of the game. We need to look at our game plans and assess whether they are appropriate for the moment. We then need to deliver those plans with our depth of skills, clear, unemotional decision-making and precise execution. And we know from our past experiences that if we continue to deliver this approach we can win games from any position.

The real key to managing expectations is being able to arrest the emotional engagement in expectations. In cricket, there are different ways for this to occur. We have structured breaks in play that allow us to emotionally and physically remove ourselves from the environment, and then take some brief time to reset our plans and mental approach.

When breaks in play are not available to the team or individual, the situation requires intervention from a team leader. Generally this will be the captain, vice-captain or coach. However, the opportunity resides within the make-up and dynamics of the side for any person to provide such leadership.

Each individual can, and mostly does, take ownership of situations themselves. It is a very difficult process for a player totally involved in the contest to take emotional control of his actions in response to not meeting, meeting or exceeding expectations. This particular characteristic is an important feature of great players and great teams. Such a response is often referred to as *composure* — being able to make quality decisions at moments of intense competition. Inextricably tied into these moments are the expectations of what the outcomes should be.

Expectations can be a constant source of support as well as distraction. Provided the team and individuals are vigilant these emotional interferences can be managed quite well.

KEY MESSAGES

1. There are two types of expectations — *internal*, those which you can control, and *external*, those which you cannot control.

2. Spend time and energy understanding how you can best control your *internal expectations*.

3. Use strategies such as key words or phrases, and/or briefly removing yourself from the situation to reset you goals and see what you need to do next.

4. Intervention from team leaders or the coach, selector, or a specialist advisor can bring objectivity to a decision that needs to be made.

11

Change

Nothing is more certain than uncertainty ... and nothing is more constant than change.

SOMEBODY SEEMS TO BE winding all the clocks forward so that they go a little bit faster every day; each week, each month and each year seems to be going faster than the one before.

Along with this feeling of living at a faster pace, it seems that we are also having to deal with a faster rate of change. Whether it's through computer technology, climate change, the globalisation of all that we do, scientific advances or just day-to-day changes in the cost of living, we are having to deal with a change phenomena that is more pronounced than any previous generation has faced.

Human beings are mostly very predictable. We like to operate in our comfort zones. Most of us like to see the world remain the way it is — to remain certain we can bank on it.

Anything that hints at changing how we view the world is generally greeted with a degree of scepticism. However, history has proven that the human race is very creative, inventive and innovative. Sometimes this is born out of need or crisis, sometimes by accident and other times by a long methodical process. Change then, is always with us.

The whole change process is a complicated one — particularly when an organisation or a team and its individuals are very set in their ways. My view on change is that there are a whole lot of interconnecting forces that can ultimately bring about change. But it depends upon the strength of each force on the overall operation of the team that determines how long the change process will take.

Some of these forces are externally driven, such as the *environment* in which we operate. For example, the way the Australian Cricket Team thinks, prepares, plays and conducts its daily life is far different when it tours India than when it is playing at home.

A *crisis* is probably the greatest catalyst for change and that generally resides outside the control of the organisation. For example, the drought that had been ravaging many parts of the country in early 2006, including my home in South-east Queensland, was severely threatening the living standards of the capital city, Brisbane. The consequences of this included a state of emergency being declared, an election held, a grand plan for water storage and retention developed, and a raft of changes to the way water was being used implemented.

Like expectations, change can be both internal and external. External changes are events over which we have little or no control, whereas internal change are things we can exert more control over.

The major elements of internal change are:

- Cultural change.

- Systems change.

- Change agents.

- Individual change.

Cultural change is an ongoing task for any team or organisation. It involves all the people within the team, the people who surround the team (i.e. in other sections of the organisation), the people who make key decisions for the organisation, and those who reside at the top of the organisation, such as the Board and CEO.

Cultural change affects the way the organisation and its people go about their daily work and influences how they deliver daily messages of what their team and ultimately their organisation is all about — that is how they present their *values* and *principles*.

Supporting the people in performing their daily routines are the systems and processes of the organisation. And these systems and processes need to be in sync with what the organisation and the people within the organisation profess to be... or want to be.

Then there are the *change agents* — those persons (or sometimes systems) who are introduced to bring about change.

I have always seen my role as a change agent, and I think I am not too far wrong in saying that is why my former employers such as Queensland Cricket, the Middlesex County Cricket

Club and Cricket Australia gave me the opportunity to coach their teams.

However, as an employer, if one does not really appreciate the role of the change agent and its potential impact on the organisation as a whole — not simply the specific team that is being coached — then it can lead to significant conflict, frustration and anger for all parties.

By way of example, let me tell you about the role I played in implementing a range of changes with the Queensland Cricket organisation. Firstly I believed there needed to be a major cultural shift. As previously discussed, Queensland had not won the Sheffield Shield since it was admitted to the competition in 1926, although it had come perilously close on a number of occasions. As each year went by the mythical reasons for Queensland's failure grew, along with the haunting ghosts of tragedies of the past.

The culture change had already begun with a major change to the marketing of the Queensland team. It had been renamed as the Queensland Bulls and aligned itself to the power, strength and symbolism of a charging bull of the Santa Gertrudis variety. Stuart Law, one of the younger players, had also been made captain.

These changes were followed with my appointment by Queensland Cricket, who took a brave new step in appointing a coach who did not have a long and successful playing career at either international or at first-class level. I then further implemented change by speaking about Queensland's future directions in terms of systems and processes, not about winning!

Change

I always saw my job as getting the right systems and processes in place so that Queensland could dominate the Australian domestic cricket competition for the next decade. If I was successful in getting these things in place, then sometime down the track we would win that Holy Grail — the Sheffield Shield. So I constantly looked at our systems and processes of planning, training, communication, behaviour, rewards, team hierarchy, support staff and so on.

Communication was also a major feature of change. New elements of communication included computer analysis of the players' performances and feedback, personal and team goal setting, and social communication.

The final change lay in the *individuals* themselves. Again, I was fortunate to have a fairly stable group of players who were also reasonably young. The only regular Australian team players were Ian Healy and Craig McDermott, who were around intermittently. The former Australian captain, Allan Border, who had retired from international cricket, was set to give one full year for Queensland.

There was plenty of experience amongst the senior players but they had also been scarred many a time over previous seasons, none more so than Carl Rackemann. And others like Trevor Barsby, Dirk Tazelaar and Greg Rowell had also felt the pain of dashed hopes, aspirations and expectations one too many times.

So it was time to give our experienced players an injection of new life: different training regimes and routines of which we were all expected to be a part; greater responsibilities for some in off-field decisions about dress, travel, accommodation and social events; more detailed and precise preparation through meetings and accompanying visual and data analysis; and the selection of the right staff to deliver these messages practically.

Besides the more impersonal elements of change such as systems and process management, and the less visible, slow moving component of cultural management, there was a change in the way we went about creating a legacy for the remainder of the decade. Our younger players were the key element to this change. So the likes of Jimmy Maher, Martin Love, Matthew Hayden, Michael Kasprowicz, Andy Bichel, Wade Seccombe, Adam Dale, Geoff Foley, Andrew Symonds, Matthew Mott and Scott Muller were not only part of our squads, but also very much encouraged to challenge, question, interact and listen to their senior counterparts.

There was to be no structured hierarchy. Individuals accorded each other respect based on a range of factors without having any artificial distinction based on seniority. Herein lay the foundation for change to the present for a new-look and successful future.

Queensland was very fortunate to have this mix of people and players at the same time that other significant changes were occurring. I am sure that if you asked board members about that era, they would tell you it was a shining example of how to instigate and sustain organisational change!

KEY MESSAGES

1. Accept change as inevitable.

2. Understand that external change is generally uncontrollable.

3. Use key elements of internal change, which are: cultural, systems and processes, change agent(s) and individual.

4. The coordination of these will dictate the speed of change.

12

Leadership

I FIRMLY BELIEVE THAT the capacity of leadership is in everyone.

However, not everyone is seen as a leader. We tend to think of a leader as a person who holds a designated or formal position — a manager in business, a party or faction leader in politics, a minister of religion, a figurehead in the community, a captain or coach in sport and so on.

How often do we sit back and wait, and let someone else make a decision for us? The sheep mentality! It's a safe option. But it's also a decision from which we learn little — particularly about ourselves.

In the main, most people are satisfied with this arrangement as it means they don't have to be the ones to make decisions on behalf of others; they don't have to take on additional responsibilities; they're not forced to make decisions which will make them unpopular with some sections of the community; and they can happily find a target to blame when the decisions made don't suit them.

As I said, *leadership is in everyone;* and this is a key principle in terms of the Australian Cricket Team' ssuccess.Without all the team members subscribing to this principle, then we would have players and people within the team who rely on the decisions of others. A team comprising such individuals will always play conservatively and not be courageous. They will make decisions that reduce risk, and they will attempt not to lose first and foremost.

Let me describe cricket in its simplest terms. Cricket is a 'one-ball' game. Each player, be they batter, bowler or fielder, is required to respond to the circumstances of only one ball at a time. And the team requires the player to make the highest quality decision — then repeat these high quality decisions one ball after one ball after one ball and so on.

In every one of these moments the individual is the 'team leader'. The Australian Cricket Team performs consistently well because the captain and the team place confidence and belief in each individual to make a quality decision on that one ball. Equally, each individual seeks this position of leadership. As a consequence, the majority of challenges that the team faces are ones that we have not only faced, but conquered, through the decision making (the leadership capacity) of all members in and around the team. It is not just the designated leader who is charged with the responsibility, it is everyone.

Of course, this makes logical sense in sport as the captain cannot be in every place at every moment. A cricket captain cannot be involved with every ball of the game. They cannot be involved with every decision affecting the management of the team. So they need to back the judgement of each individual within the team — coaches, players, support staff, selectors and administrators. The captain needs and wants these people to lead.

In the Australian Cricket Team, leadership is actively encouraged by providing everyone with opportunities to demonstrate leadership skills. Examples of this process are Ricky Ponting requiring players to tell him during the course of the game what *the moment needs;* having an individual player lead group discussion on game tactics and current team issues; formal and informal presentations by individuals to the media; and staff taking responsibility and leadership for specialised areas of training, physical preparation, tactical analysis and so on.

This approach is no different from a CEO or a small business owner who wants every member of their staff that deals with a customer to act like a leader of the organisation, and make a quality decision on behalf of the 'team'.

Leadership styles vary depending on personality. Steve Waugh liked to lead by example, especially when the situation was more difficult than the norm. He would steel himself for battle and dared, taunted and defied the opposition. He implored his troops to play aggressively. There was only winning or losing, drawing was never part of the plan. This approach was possible due to the high level of skills of the Australian Cricket Team as demonstrated by the result of sixteen straight Test match wins.

As Steve entered the latter years of his captaincy, his leadership combined with a profile of statesmanship. In India he helped to establish a centre for orphaned young girls. He was a prolific writer and had an increased media presence, all of which gave him an elevated persona.

His brother Mark, on the other hand, did not occupy any formal leadership position within the team. I think he definitely had leadership aspirations, but these became somewhat suffocated beside Steve's ambitions and achievements. Nevertheless, Mark was still an influential leader within the team ranks due to his exceptional skills, which were clearly demonstrated over many years. Leadership was also accorded to him because of his astute cricket brain, and his personality and humour around the group.

Ricky Ponting, who has succeeded Steve Waugh as captain, has a similar leadership approach — leading from the front, aggressively. He is a very tough competitor. However, while he mirrors the 'Waugh-like' aggression, he tempers this approach with the knowledge that one's strength is also one's weakness.

Ricky's leadership style is more inclusive with his senior players. He makes sure that they make the necessary input into team decisions. He also makes sure that all the team members are aware of his decisions, and that everyone is clear what he expects as a result.

His leadership since the Ashes defeat in England 2005 has been one of the factors that has taken the Australian Cricket Team to its current position. Leadership, especially formal leadership, does not happen overnight. The person must learn to understand the job, the responsibilities and how those responsibilities impact on both their personal and professional life. There is a definite learning curve, and Ricky has accelerated his progress along this evolutionary curve.

Adam Gilchrist, who has only had the chance to lead Australia in six Test matches, is no less determined than Ricky. He has the 'nice guy' leadership style, not wanting to create conflict with any member of the team, and creating an atmosphere where that is reciprocated. He has been an unbelievable second in charge and has shown exceptional leadership qualities in providing immense support for his captain, Ricky.

Other senior members of the team vary in the way they conduct themselves as leaders. Shane Warne wears his heart on his sleeve. He is very passionate about what he believes and is therefore quite outspoken in style. While his approach occasionally brings him into conflict with the thoughts and opinions of others, the team usually benefits.

Glenn McGrath leads simply by doing. He has a simple formula for performing and, provided he does not complicate this approach with mischief or being 'caught up' in the emotions of an event, he is 'Mr Reliable'. In his twilight years he adopted a father figure role to the young guns of Australian fast bowling — a role from which Brett Lee, Shane Watson, Mitch Johnson, Shaun Tait, Nathan Bracken and Ben Hilfenhaus all benefited.

In structuring a team that champions leadership, the environment created by the formal leadership team — captain and coach — allows everyone to lead. As Steve Waugh has said: 'Smart leaders show faith in the people they have surrounded themselves with and rely on them to help the leader out.'

KEY MESSAGES

1. Leadership needs to be a key value of any team.

2. Everyone has the capacity to lead.

3. Good leaders provide everyone in their team with the opportunities to lead and to learn from their leadership experiences.

4. Everyone has their own personal leadership style.

13

Mental toughness

WHEN ASKED WHY THE Australian cricket team has dominated international competition for such a long period of time, the answers are many. The team has great talent in its ranks; as a whole it has a great self-belief (an inner arrogance); it has an excellent system of support staff around the team; it has a very good talent discrimination process through the domestic cricket program; and it has a wide range of traditions which are passed on to each 'new cap'.

There are other factors that contribute to the success of the team, but one that helps to make all of the above a reality is *mental toughness.*

What does the term actually mean?

For me, it is the ability of the individual at a given moment to make the highest quality decision for himself and therefore for his team. Furthermore, mental toughness is the ability to make such decisions consistently, time after time after time.

Mental toughness

Steve Waugh has described mental toughness as 'the ability to give 100 per cent attention to the ball he is about to face, then do it next ball, and the next'.

But is it so important?

Clearly, where a decision or a series of decisions has an immediate impact on the performance of an individual, then the ability to make *consistent* quality decisions is crucial. Within the team context, the sum of the answers (or decisions) made by individuals to the 'questions' constantly being asked by the opposition corresponds to the overall team response to the game.

Obviously, if a player or players can achieve this state over an extended period of time it has significant ramifications for the outcome of a match. In addition, if one can replicate this outside the sporting arena, then it can have great applicability to our daily working, social and emotional lives.

So how does one obtain this state of mental toughness?

I believe we can conceptualise this state a little easier if we think of the mind having a series of *compartments*. What I think mentally tough athletes do very well is to *compartmentalise* aspects of their life. That is, there is a cricket compartment which is filled with sub-compartments such as batting, captaincy, scoreboard/state of game, fielding, bowling and so on. Alongside the cricket compartment there are other compartments, such as family, friends, business interests, holidays and free time. Each compartment then has many sub-compartments.

Arriving at a training session or at the ground for game day, mentally tough cricketers open the cricket component and lock off all other, unnecessary compartments. This allows them to remove themselves from everything else but the task at hand. This then allows them to examine which cricket sub-compartments will be needed for that particular match that particular day.

Shane Warne is an easy example of this process. There is always so much happening in his life, some good, some not so good, that often the cricket ground is his refuge as well as his stage. The dressing rooms become a sanctuary, a safe environment away from all other parts of his life. Stepping through the dressing room door is like the actor preparing himself for the next show. As he walks onto the field, he has, on most occasions, found the sub-compartments of cricket he needs. He is ready to play out the drama of the day using only the sub-compartments he needs, when he needs them. He knows each of these sub-compartments carry all the answers, all the tricks, all the experience, all the skills he needs — providing he stays with them and does not allow himself to become distracted into other compartments.

I saw this process acted out by the 'Ice Man' himself, Steve Waugh. It was my first tour with the Australian team and we were playing New Zealand in Auckland in an ODI. The game was meandering along and we were in a pretty comfortable position. Steve was next in and we were all on the balcony watching proceedings. However, we were still within earshot of the spectators.

A spectator made a remark to which Steve quickly reacted. This action took me by surprise — why would Steve, the most 'mentally tough' cricketer on the planet, be bothered by a harmless call from a spectator? Their verbal jousting continued and became relatively animated — why bother? I thought. A wicket fell and Steve strode off as if he was confronting an enemy. So here was the reason why he had bothered to engage in a verbal dispute with the spectator. It helped him to unlock the compartment he needed to perform with the bat. He needed to face an enemy, an angry enemy, an enemy that was making life tough for him and the team, an enemy that he needed to overcome. The spectator just happened to be a symbol, a means to his batting compartment which told him that he played his best cricket when Australia had its backs to the wall. Steve created this situation as he strode through the crowd.

I saw the reverse side of this compartmentalisation skill in Steve when we toured South Africa in March 2002. He had just been dropped as captain of the Australian ODI team; however, he remained as captain of the Test team — a difficult role for anyone to fulfil.

Steve struggled with his Test performances that tour. The reason for his poor form lay in the fact that he had not come to terms with being dropped by the selectors from the captaincy of the one-day team. He still believed he was good enough to lead Australia to the next World Cup in South Africa, twelve months away, after being one of the heroes of the last campaign in England in 1999. He was unable to lock off a number of compartments.

So when he batted, he had his normal batting compartment open, but his skills, experience, and confidence contained within this compartment were constantly being interrupted by other compartments which contained a range of emotions.

Mental toughness or compartmentalisation is an essential state of being for athletes to reach, if they wish to compete successfully over a long period of time. It enables the athlete to 'play the moment' while being aware of all that is around them. Everything that surrounds them is not a distraction, but simply a backdrop of information which signals when and what other sub-compartment should be unlocked.

KEY MESSAGES

1. Fill each compartment with appropriate knowledge, skills and confidence.

2. Know exactly how to unlock a compartment.

3. In order to deal with the present have only the correct compartment(s) open.

14

Planning

THERE ARE TIMES WHEN our lives seem to be totally consumed by planning — house plans, holiday plans, family plans, strategic business plans and financial plans.

There's no doubt that whatever we do, it has some element of planning to it. For those of us who like a little more certainty, we are forever making lists of what needs to be done, when and by whom. For others, such a regimented way of life is not for them. Yet, as hard as they may try to deny it, such people do have some sort of plan as to what is important in their lives and what they see as priorities.

Within the Australian Cricket Team, there is a similar mixture of personalities. For instance, Matthew Hayden thinks very carefully about his opposition, the type of bowling he will face, where they have bowled to him previously, and how the conditions will affect batting against them. With this clear picture in mind — his 'game plan' — he then sets about his preparation for the game carefully, and wherever possible meticulously, structuring his batting practice sessions to mirror the game scenarios he will face. Therefore, once the game commences he is prepared for what the game will throw at him, knowing that his extensive preparation (as well as his long-time experience) will stand him in good stead to respond to all challenges.

Most of the Australian batsmen have similar plans for their preparation, although they will have different methods in which they achieve that final goal of being ready to play — technically, physically, mentally and tactically. Even Andrew Symonds, who prefers to occupy that end of the planning spectrum which is more impromptu, has discovered that to be able to be himself through the course of a game, he needs to structure his preparation in such a way that he enters the cricket arena filled with confidence in his own abilities to deal with his opponents. Consequently, he has learnt over time exactly what he needs to do to give himself the best chance of performing — a basic game plan.

The bowlers, on the other hand, are slightly different.

Like the batters, the bowlers work backwards from where they want to be at the time they have to perform. That is, each bowler analyses the opposition in their own way — some using their years of experience (such as Warne and McGrath), some through watching detailed vision, and analysing statistics and batting patterns of opposing players (such as Bracken, Watson, Bichel and Kasprowicz). Others use group discussion, either in meetings and/or training sessions (Johnson and Stuart Clark), and then there are those who simply do what has always worked for them (Tait, Lee, Symonds and Michael Clarke). Prior to games there is generally a combination of the above for each player. The difference for the bowlers is that they do not devote the same amount of physical time to perfecting their bowling as batters do. The principal reason for this difference is that physically they are not able to subject their bodies to the same degrees of fatigue as batsmen in pursuit of honing their skills. They need a fresh body to respond to the demands of the game. They will hopefully overcome any technical deficiencies through employment of strong mental and tactical skills. This is where the likes of Warne and McGrath excel.

But herein lies the essence of planning:

- Everyone does it and needs it, but it has to be in a format/method with which they are comfortable.

- It provides the individual or organisation with a reference framework.

- The framework provides great flexibility in its methodology.

- The framework provides a ready means for assessment, review and improvements.

The elements to any plan are:

- A vision — something which takes the game to another level.

- Aims — the elements to achieving this vision.

- Measurable goals — a measure of what achieving each element means.

- New challenges — identifying new methods to be adopted.

An overall team plan needs to be developed by the key stakeholders, such as the coaches, support staff, captain and vice-captain. There are many ways to produce such a plan, ranging from total consultation (every person for whom the plan may have some meaning or impact is given the opportunity to express opinions) to no consultation (the plan is owned and driven by one person).

My experience shows that the best way to achieve a meaningful plan is to be flexible. Everybody needs to feel they have been included or at least have had the opportunity to have their say, whether they have taken that opportunity or not. At the same time the more people who have an input the longer the plan takes to produce; the impact is lessened because time has eroded the excitement of what it is and how it will affect each individual, and the overall direction of the plan can be lost, or at best watered down from the original intent.

The following plan (see page 98) formed the basis of the way we were thinking as a playing and off-field support group for a couple of years leading into the 2007 World Cup tournament. If nothing else, to have many people thinking about being *the best-skilled team the world has ever seen* was a mindset that greatly assisted our performance once we arrived in the Windies. We certainly did not achieve all our aims and goals — but we were always driving towards them.

WORLD CUP 2007 CHALLENGE

To be the best-skilled team the world has ever seen

THE PLAN

1. We must have the highest standards of *defensive plans and skills* (i.e. set new standards in terms of bowling and fielding strategies combined with the ability to execute those plans consistently under pressure).

2. We must be the most *athletic* team (i.e. minimise any athletic disadvantage we currently have within the squad and/or maximise the athletic advantage we have over teams).

3. We must *bat with an approach* that allows full expression of the team's skills (i.e. develop batsmen who are good decision makers and physically execute their skills at various times during the game under pressure).

4. We must set new standards in levels of professionalism on and off the field.

Defensive Plans And Skills — Bowling

- To be able to bowl on average 55% dot balls per match. To do this, bowlers need to be able to deliver the three lengths consistently and under pressure (range of yorkers, top of off, bouncer).

- All bowlers need to have knowledge of individual batsmen and skills to bowl wicket taking and dot balls to each.

- Bowlers to have the skills to bowl during the Power Play periods and during the last ten to fifteen overs.

- All quick and medium quick bowlers must be able to deliver the following on demand: range of yorkers, bouncers, normal and reverse swing, range of slower balls and use of angles at crease.

- Spinners to be able to deliver on demand the following: various degrees of turn, range of pace and trajectory changes and use of angles at crease. All spinners must also be able to deliver yorker length deliveries at will.

- The team must develop a signal system between bowler, keeper, captain and all fieldsmen for particular plays.

- Bowlers must position themselves in their follow through wherever possible to force batsmen to run around them.

Defensive Plans And Skills — Fielding

- Fielding is the second part to the defensive plan but will play a key role.

- Our overall target is to maintain our opportunities taken at the following standards:

  - 100% Grade 1 chances — regulation catches.

  - 80% of Grade 2 chances — increased degree of difficulty, but expect to take.

  - 50% of Grade 3 chances — difficult chances, dives, one-handed.

- A movement rating will also be developed to measure runs saved, extra efforts, dive stops and assists.

- Fielders are encouraged to throw at the stumps at all times to support play, must be active at all times to prevent over throws.

To Be The Most Athletic Team

- All players must improve personal bests in speed, agility and power tests.

- Players will specialise in inner and outer ring fielding positions, but have the physical and technical skills to field in most positions.

- Players will improve speed between wickets and improve their turning skills and physical abilities.

- Players need to be able to use non-preferred side for underarm throwing.

Offensive Plans — Batting

- The overall target of our batting team is a minimum of 60% scoring shots.

- Batsmen will have the ability to score on both sides of the wicket off the front and back foot against both slow and quick bowlers in variable match and wicket conditions.

- Batsmen to have a range of shots including ranges of power, skill to take pace off the ball to skill and power to hit the ball over the boundary.

- Batsmen to develop the ability to use the crease and manipulate the field to suit the team's and the individual's needs.

- Basic running between wicket techniques to be fine tuned (backing up, straight line running, turning, staying in close to stumps for spinners as well as running on best surface).

- Batsmen to have flexibility to bat anywhere in order, and consequently with different partners at different times in the match.

- Batsmen will be very knowledgeable about opposition bowlers and team tactics.

Best Organised Team

- All preparations to be completed before leaving for WC 2007 (e.g. playing manual, opposition profiles, equipment, supplies and media, etc.).

- All contingencies to be understood with plans in place to manage.

- Training — skills, physical, recovery to be *best practice*.

- Downtime team activities to be planned and both organised and flexible.

NEW Action Items That Arise From The Plan

- Signal system — this option to be further developed with team leadership group. Also the option of developing *Phases of Play* that all players are aware of (almost set plays that cover periods of time, rather than just one ball).

- Organised — alternative training formats to be investigated and trialled prior to World Cup. This may include training without use of nets, for example.

KEY MESSAGES

1. Accept planning as an integral process to successful performance.

2. Planning is simply a reference framework that allows great flexibility in methodology.

3. Any plan must have shared ownership by all parties that will be affected by it.

15

The big three

*On track with a mix of the 'didn't happen', a touch of the
unplanned and a dash of Murphy's law for good measure.*

PLANNING FOR THE 2007 World Cup received a real boost with the
2005 Ashes loss against England. It made all of us — Cricket
Australia, the players and support staff — take stock of what
had happened. More importantly, the result tilled the soil of
change.

Cricket Australia freed up the purse strings somewhat to allow
much needed support resources to be directed towards the team.
Players took greater responsibility for the outcomes of the Ashes,
showing that a dented and bruised pride (that is, pride in their
performance as individuals and collectively as the Australian
Cricket Team) is a powerful catalyst for drawing together a
unit which had in some ways been disjointed for the previous
six months.

And it made me stop and ask myself three important
questions:

1. Can I still make a difference with this team — not just an incremental impact, but something significant?

2. Even if I believe I can, do I still have the energy, motivation and desire to keep driving change?

3. Do I still have the respect of the players, at least the vast majority of them?

If my answer to any of these questions had been 'No', I wouldn't have re-signed after the Ashes and made the commitment to stay with Cricket Australia until the end of the World Cup in 2007. By then I knew that after completion of the World Cup, which would be a culmination of a lot of travel, tours and three major tests including the ICC Champions Trophy and the 2006-07 Ashes series in Australia, I would have to answer 'No' to questions one and two. Hence, at the end of the World Cup in the West Indies in April 2007, it would be time for retirement.

So once we had played the super series against the Rest of the World in late 2005, the vision I wanted Cricket Australia, the players and support staff to buy was the concept of the *Big Three*: the ICC Trophy which we had never won, the 2006-07 Ashes which we were seeking to regain and the World Cup, which would give us three World Cups in a row.

The concept was about elevating this period in Australian cricket to an unprecedented level, such that whatever I asked for was provided. That meant coaching staff for the team, new equipment, a camp that would physically and mentally challenge all contracted players, some radical training clothing produced by our new sponsor, Adidas, for display at the World Cup, schedule changes to allow for targeted preparation for the three majors instead of minor matches or tournaments, and for players to gear themselves for the long term as well as short term — that is, to understand that the bigger picture will sometimes get in the road of the need to deal with the present.

I didn't achieve everything I wanted — a continual source of frustration in my role. But I think I did achieve a certain elevation of urgency, necessary for this period in Australian cricket history.

With this in mind, I presented my vision for the One-Day International (ODI) team — to arrive at the World Cup as the 'best-skilled team the world had seen'. Therefore, everything that we did as a team — technical, physical, tactical and mental skills training — was designed to chase this dream.

While this planning and preparation was underway from October 2005 to April 2007, we had to deal with a home-and-away Test series against South Africa, a Tri-series against Sri Lanka and South Africa, a further series of ODIs against South Africa in South Africa and, finally, a Test and ODI series against Bangladesh on its home pitch. We survived this period pretty well — we won seven of eight Tests and drew the other, won the ODI Tri-series, lost the ODI series in South Africa after losing the final match at the Wanderers Stadium in Johannesburg even after making the world record total of 434, and then won the ODI series in Bangladesh.

There was time to gather breath before our next engagement in August 2006 in Kuala Lumpur, Malaysia — the DLF Cup

Tri-series against India and the West Indies. But plenty of wheels were turning behind the scenes with deliberations on selections. We were trying to project forward to the World Cup and decide the type of game/strategy we wanted to use, and therefore the type of players we would require. On top of that there was the continual revising of budgets and plans for all the resources (people, equipment and scheduling), and constant thinking about all the permutations and combinations that would influence our World Cup performance.

As I said the concept was the *Big Three*, so before entering the final phases of World Cup preparation, we had the ICC Champions Trophy in India to negotiate, and then the 'minor' matter of the Ashes to deal with from late November to early January.

We climbed both those mountains successfully.

Then it was time to shift our full attention to the one day team and what we needed to do to get our selves ready for the World Cup. As with all projects there is a need to:

- Have a clear vision and stick to it.
- Deal with the present, although there is always a risk it may be compromised by the future.
- Keep everyone within the team clear on what is being done, even though they might not agree with it.
- Absorb the inevitable external criticisms.

Our overall objectives for the final training period before departure for the World Cup were:

- Finalise our 15-man squad by providing all possible players with a last chance to make selection.

- Undertake some additional physical work so it would provide a better base for the World Cup.

- Establish our preferred playing strategies.

- Ensure our entire squad was as physically and mentally prepared as could be expected prior to leaving.

- Rest key players where necessary through the lower priority tournaments of the Commonwealth Bank Series in Australia and the Chappell-Hadlee Series in New Zealand.

- Have our game tested to identify where there were weak points so these could be addressed leading into the Cup.

By adopting these methods, we did compromise our playing performances through both home ODI series. Players were lethargic at times due to increased travel (where we provided for extra time at home), and an increased workload coming into a game. Key players were not played at times as their selections were certain for the World Cup, while those who were trying to press their claims were given additional opportunities. We suffered three serious injuries to Andrew Symonds, Matthew Hayden and Brett Lee (which ultimately ruled him out of selection) and a number of less serious but nonetheless concerning niggles to Ricky Ponting, Stuart Clark, Shane Watson and Glenn McGrath, despite taking all precautions.

After winning our first four games of the Commonwealth Bank Series in Australia comfortably, I knew we were gaining a false impression of where our game was at. Simply, New Zealand

and England were not providing us with the competition we needed. So I said this publicly, as much for our players as well as hopefully inciting some reaction from our opposition. I needed our players to know that our results were inflated and that other teams around the world would be much tougher.

We won three of our next four games, but New Zealand improved significantly with the inclusion of a few of their regular team members, and so too did a resurgent England. In fact, England won the two finals games despite us being in winning positions in both. Having batted first in Melbourne, we were unable to sustain the start we had and could not restrict the run chase. While in Sydney, we were able to rectify our defence somewhat to keep England to a very gettable score, but then our batting disintegrated at the top, leaving us well short of their total.

We travelled to New Zealand without Ponting, Gilchrist, Michael Clarke and Symonds to play a concertinaed three-game series — and we soon lost Lee. We had also brought Watson back into the series, knowing full well he was below match readiness, but thought that these matches would be invaluable preparation for him in the weeks ahead. By this time New Zealand had their full squad, had been at home for nearly two weeks and were ready to use these games as their final preparations for the World Cup. For our part, we wanted to arrest the losses and return home with that winning feeling again.

New Zealand's preparedness and the loss of key players, as well as the crammed travel and playing schedule, all contributed to us losing all three games — even though for two of the games, we were again in winning positions. But the biggest contribution to these losses, as well as those in Australia, was that in at least three of the five games we didn't maximise our batting totals, while in four of the five cases our bowling defence didn't make consistently good decisions and/or execute those decisions.

Now it was certainly not in the grand plan to head to the World Cup losing five games in a row. It was certainly not intended to give all other contenders for the World Cup a boost, seeing Australia being beaten. And the performances were certainly not designed to give the perennial critics like Ian Chappell, Bobby Simpson and other former Test players extra space in their newspaper columns for their normal vitriol.

We returned from New Zealand battered and bruised. Egos were damaged. The chairman of selectors, Ricky Ponting and myself had a series of phone calls wondering whether our overall objectives had been correct. Our administrative bosses were ringing to consult me immediately after we lost games — calls that reverberated the single question: 'What the hell is going on?'

However, despite the spate of lost games, I still believed we had achieved a lot of what was needed to take us to the World Cup. And this was my constant message publicly and privately.

My real concern, though, was the injuries. Brett Lee was out of the tournament — one of our leading strike bowlers, an outstanding athlete and a more than capable hitter. Taking Andrew Symonds to the World Cup was a big gamble with the risk that his shoulder would blow out again. Michael Clarke was still carrying a worrisome hip injury, which prevented him from specialist throwing practice and impeded his bowling. Matthew Hayden had a broken toe and badly bruised instep, compliments of his record-breaking last innings in New Zealand. The old pro, 'Pidgeon' McGrath plus counterpart Stuart Clark were both having continuing niggles — the product of age and the effects of bowling and travel on the body by the end of a long season of cricket. It effectively meant that the vision of arriving at the World Cup as 'the best-skilled team the world has ever seen' was no longer possible. If we were to wrestle other teams for this World Cup, rather than dominate, then we would need to be very smart about using the skills we brought.

But I knew we had done the planning. I knew we had done our preparation. I knew we had the skills in the team to perform very well. I knew we had the leadership in Ricky, Adam, Glenn, Matthew Hayden and Andrew Symonds. I knew we had 'gamers' in Haddin, Hodge, Clark, Clarke and Hogg. I knew we had match-winning potential in Watson, Johnson, Bracken and Tait. I knew we had an excellent support team for the playing squad.

So I left for the World Cup a little shaken and not surprised by where our weaknesses had been exposed, but very excited about trying to pull all the pieces together in time to make the semi-finals. If we could get there, then anything could happen!

KEY MESSAGES

1. While not totally ignoring all the noise that surrounds the preparation for a major project, make sure your *filters* are working overtime so that you can stick to the plan.

2. Spend time keeping other significant stakeholders on track as well, since they will be subject to the same or similar *noise invasion* as you.

3. The present may need to be compromised or sacrificed for the final outcome of the project.

16

World Cup

Puttin' the pieces together.

WINNING AN EVENT SUCH as the World Cup requires many things to come together simultaneously. Some are controllable and some are not. And within what is controllable, there is a need to prioritise what is more important at different times to keep the project on track.

One of the controllable factors is *experience* and how it can be used beneficially for the current event. The experience of competing in such a tournament means that some players and some support staff have an understanding of the winning, the hard work, the travel, the boredom, the controversies, the media speculation, the highs and lows of team-mates, the humour, the life education that is involved.

This experience was brought to bear on the planning of the early part of the tour, as the previous campaign had shown us that a good start to a tour through training, playing and coming together as a group helped significantly in our early progression through the tournament. The idea of tournament progression is not to be playing at your best from the first game, because this is unsustainable for the eight or nine weeks prior to the finals. Rather, the team needs to isolate games for which it aims to play as well as it can, so that, through a gradual process of winning and improving, the momentum and confidence builds as the team progresses to the most important games at the back end of the World Cup.

In 2003, we had set up our base in the little university town of Potchefstroom, in the country just outside the bright lights of Johannesburg. Here we trained well; we had most of a small hotel to ourselves and had it functioning for our purposes, and we set up our commitments to each other for the tour. We identified that the first two games of that tournament were crucial as we played Pakistan then India. Both teams were potential semi-finalists. We managed to get across the line against Pakistan and then demolished India, so our quest for the trophy had begun according to plan.

For 2007, we were allocated the sleepy little island in the Grenadines called St Vincents — possibly better known for its link to the nearby island retreats of some of the rich and famous such as Oprah Winfrey and Mick Jagger than its rating as a world cricket destination. The Sunset Shores resort — with a taste of calypso licence to the word 'resort' — was our home for the first ten days or so, and where we would play our warm-up games. We had sent our assistant coach, Dene Hills, ahead in January to ascertain what we needed to do to make this stage of the tour (and our next two island stops) more comfortable and more practical for our needs. St Vincents was to be our new Potchefstroom. It is here that *puttin' the pieces together* really began, with everyone getting used to the pace of the Windies people, and beginning to deal with the vagaries of training and movement around the island.

Experience also determines how individuals and a team cope with distractions and expectations. Those who have been around the international scene for a while know that one of the potential distractions is the stories that the media write. It is something over which we generally have little control, but there is no doubt that it has an impact on a player, coach or team when the media ravenously, if not factually, pursues a story.

Routines and maintaining good personal habits for physical training, diet, rest, recovery and rehabilitation are essential for players to perform well on tours. And while we place faith in the majority of players having the best intentions in this regard, there are many location and logistical obstacles to this occurring. Hence we have a support structure around the team to eliminate most of these hurdles. These include a personal trainer, physiotherapist, masseuse, security officer, local liaison officer and media manager. For an event such as the World Cup we looked carefully at the most appropriate time for the team's partners and families to be part of the World Cup campaign. This was early in the tour in a beautiful resort called The Marriott in St Kitts. And while there is no prohibition of partners joining their husbands or boyfriends, experience shows that it is preferable at the business end of the tour for everyone to have one clear focus — playing their best cricket.

Controversies are always part and parcel of such an event, which has the attention of at least the cricket world. In 2003, the Australian team faced one of the biggest stories with Shane Warne pulling out of the event the night before our first game due to a positive drugs test for using diuretics. In 2007, the World Cup was marked by the huge logistical problem of moving teams around the islands, but then was plunged into crisis with the death of Pakistan's coach, Bob Woolmer, immediately after their loss to Ireland and early elimination from the Cup. Bob's death was one of the saddest days for cricket and elite sport.

Preparation and team cohesion are two other very important factors that can be controllable and are always at the forefront of our priorities. In terms of preparation we constantly monitor:

- The training needs of our squad (not as scientifically or with as much fine detail as football teams) and how we can most effectively and efficiently provide those needs.

- The schedule and how best to structure our skills work and additional physical training.

- The opposition we are to play.

- The venues on which we are to play.

Our preparation in this tournament included warm-up games against Zimbabwe and England in St Vincents, plus our first two games of the tournament proper against Scotland and the Netherlands.

World Cup

With regard to team cohesion there was a need for me to recognise that:

- We did not arrive in the Windies as the best-skilled team the world has ever seen; however, we were still a very skilled team.

- We had many first-timers at the World Cup and some players such as Shaun Tait, Brad Hodge and Brad Haddin, had not been part of the ICC Trophy team.

- Everyone, apart from our security officer and masseuse, had been part of our pre-season boot camp.

- We had a much bigger and more diverse support team to the playing squad.

Consequently, my first meeting with the team was to outline a framework for the tour. I developed an acronym, **S.P.O.C.E.**, that stood for:

S **smart**, needing to be smart in everything we do on and off the field to allow us to bring our full resources and talents to each game.

P **preparation**, ensuring that we are fully prepared technically, physically, mentally and tactically for each game.

O **one game**, dealing only with the game we were to play in order to play as well as we can, and begin to develop a winning confidence and momentum in the tournament.

C **camp**, bringing the lessons learnt, the disciplines and the values we shared during boot camp.

E **enjoyment**, making certain that we all spent time enjoying the tour, the Windies, the wins and each other's company.

My mind was still foggy when I put this acronym together as was pointed out to me by one or two team members as I could have used SCOPE or COPES, but then I explained that was not 'spoce' to be the case ...

During this first part of the tour we did not have a full strength side: Andrew Symonds was still rehabbing his shoulder injury, along with Matthew Hayden who was nursing a broken toe and bruised instep. Adam Gilchrist was left in Australia so he could be with his family for the birth of their third child. Stuart Clark was a late addition to the team once Brett Lee's ankle injury ruled him out. The younger contingent of Michael Clarke, Shane Watson, Mitchell Johnson and Shaun Tait were all trying to make every post a winner and give themselves the best chance of being part of the 'First XI'. Ricky Ponting had not held a bat for a couple of weeks as he had not gone to New Zealand. Throw in the Sunset Shores resort, a couple of not-so-good training venues and plenty of adjustment to the pace of getting things organised, and the 'new Potchefstroom', the 2007 version, was not really working as well as it could. There was a kind of relaxed tension circulating through the team, and this needed addressing before we left the island. So, I called for a team meeting and barbecue the night before the England game.

Previously, I had been shown a fort that overlooked the harbour and so decided this was to be the venue of the team meeting. We would then adjourn back to our hotel where I had the hotel prepare a traditional Aussie barbecue. At the meeting, I had the team explain to me what the purpose of a fort was — essentially to keep out invaders — and related this to things we had to deal with like distractions, controversies and lack of discipline. Secondly, a fort is designed to protect those things that we value — friendship, loyalty, hard work and honesty.

Each player and support staff then told the group, as we nestled into one of the battlements of the fort, what they wanted to keep out during our tour, and what they wanted to keep in. These were our commitments. We briefly talked of England and what we wanted to take from the game the next day. I then presented Shane Watson with our first team award of the tour for his skill-execution during the Zimbabwe match, and finally gave everyone a team t-shirt for the tour.

Matthew Hayden took charge of the cooking when we returned and the night had achieved what was needed at this point in time, which was to lay the foundations of the tour and cement team cohesion.

KEY MESSAGES

1. Ignore experience at your peril.

2. Allow experience to provide guidance in handling expectations, distractions, controversies and maintaining routines.

3. Preparation is the passport to success.

4. Team cohesion is a long-term activity with long-term benefits.

5. To properly deal with what the present is throwing at you, prioritise key decisions and actions.

17

Mission complete

SOMETHING AKIN TO HILARY on top of Everest, Armstrong on the moon, Scott arriving at the South Pole, Australia winning a third consecutive cricket World Cup is something unparalleled in sports history. To have been a part of that journey has been an experience that will never be matched.

While the trek began eight years before the Cup in July 1999, and gained momentum in March of 2003, the final assault didn't commence until August 2006. It was at this point we put together the final pieces of the plan. We took the players and support staff on a 'boot camp' to ensure that whatever was put in front of the team (or individuals within the team), we would conquer it, we would find a way through — we would not be beaten!

Our mission was to win *The Big Three* — the ICC Trophy (never won by Australia), then the 2006-07 Ashes series (to regain the urn and completely erase the disappointing results of 2005) and finally take the treble, the 2007 World Cup.

As we strode through the early part of the tournament, a little like Rommel's Afrika Korps in the early stages of the desert war of North Africa, a number of things became clear. The strategy of having a single focus for the players had worked.

In the 2003 World Cup, I had talked to the team about the key parts of the tournament, such as the first two games against Pakistan and India. It was essential that we won those games in order to get our campaign off to a confident start, but it was also important because these were two of the teams that we could possibly meet again in the semi-finals. I also discussed why it was important to position ourselves as number one by the end of the preliminary rounds as it meant our semi-final, while not on our ideal surface, would be held at a ground we had played on at least twice before.

The 2007 Cup campaign was different. Our confidence, particularly our bowling group, had been dented by injury and the recent results in the Commonwealth Bank Series against England, and then losses to the Kiwis in the land of the long white cloud. It was crucial to have our confidence in each other returned as quickly as possible. One of the important lessons of the boot camp was that to complete a mission successfully we needed to rely on each member of the group.

I looked at the games ahead with the chairman of selectors, Andrew Hilditch and captain Ricky Ponting, and we charted the period where we were to play South Africa, West Indies and supposedly India as a make-or-break period in the tournament. For the remainder of the team, it was simply about one game at a time.

We needed to prepare for each new game the same way: arm ourselves with as much detail of the opposition as was relevant;

make our two primary groups (batting and bowling) accountable for what they would deliver through the game; ensure that we trained and prepared as hard as we could to deliver the game plan; and then play with the freedom to release those skills through quality decision making.

This approach saw Australia dominate its way through every preliminary game, no matter the strength of the opposing team or the conditions or difficulties encountered. It was with this feeling of confidence in our skills, in each other's skills, in our planning and preparation, and the surface in Barbados (a harder, faster wicket), that we could not wait for the final to arrive.

A short lead-up time is always beneficial at this stage of an event, unless there is an injury which is critical to the team. We had no serious injury problems apart from the odd niggle, but nothing that was going to prevent anyone being selected for the final contest.

We spent 25 April, Anzac day, demolishing South Africa in St Lucia, a win for which our bowling group must take great credit. Having the Proteas 5 for 27 after 9.5 overs virtually set the seal on our march through to the final.

The next day, 26 April, was a travel day and settling into the Hilton in Barbados. The day after we trained lightly, with the weather doing its best to prevent us from doing much at all. Normally we would have a final strategy meeting two days out from the game, but due to travel and the short time between games, the final team meeting was at 6.00 pm the night before the game.

We went through the various pieces of business as usual: 'administrivia' concerning the staging of anthems before the game, and a little detail of post-match requirements involving the sponsor's beer only to be drunk, no Fosters allowed; then to the playing groups who delivered their normal succinct messages and commitments to the team. Next, Ricky 'Punter' Ponting mentioned that in 2003 I had asked the team how they were feeling on the eve of the final so that individuals could express their feelings, be they confidence, doubts, nervousness, excitement or whatever. So I asked the players the same question: 'How were they feeling on the eve of the 2007 World Cup Final?'

'I can't wait,' replied Andrew 'Roy' Symonds. Michael Clarke said, 'I'm nervous, not sure I will be able to sleep. Glenn 'Pidge' McGrath answered: 'I'm very relaxed — the final is why we are here.' Punter said 'Not trying to build the game up too much.' I sensed those words were not only for himself but for the rest of the team as well. Shaun 'Taitty' Tait piped up: 'Banks beer's a good drop ... given we can't drink Fosters,' to which Brad 'Hads' Haddin replied, 'This has been your first comment in a team meeting for the whole tour!'

This light-hearted moment was followed by Punter's final address to the team as captain.

He praised the intensity of our last game against the Sri Lankans and wanted that to be repeated. He wanted the players to really enjoy the experience of playing a final, of which this was his fourth. He reinforced his total confidence in the players — no matter what they were confronted with, he knew they would be able to respond. His final message and emphasis was to have a presence on the field and in everything we did from breakfast to the end of the game.

I read the good luck fax from the Prime Minister to the team, and presented the final two team awards to Michael Hussey and Andrew Symonds. And so we left the room ready for tomorrow.

Unfortunately, inclement weather intervened just as it had in the Champions Trophy in India in October the previous year. The start was delayed, but not before Ricky had won the toss and decided to bat. Getting runs on the board first in a final is a very compelling tactic, although bad weather and the certainty that the match would be reduced in duration caused us all to rethink that strategy. In the end though, we still believed it was the best decision.

At 12.15 pm, nearly three hours after the normal commencement of play, Adam 'Gilly' Gilchrist and Matthew 'Haydos' Hayden strode to the crease to exert their presence on the final. It was a measured start with Lasith Malinga bowling his first four overs for six runs, although Gilly was getting into stride at the other end with 37 having come from Chaminda Vaas and Dilhara Fernando. The powerplay was lifted in the eleventh over and that seemed to be the signal for Gilly to really explode, taking 16 from Fernando. Captain Mahela Jayawardene introduced his trump card, Muttiah Muralitharan, and followed this with Tillakaratne Dilshan to take some pace off the ball, but still Gilly attacked, plumping Fernando back over mid-off for six to bring up the 100 partnership at 16.2 overs. Drinks were taken more for relief from Gilly's brutal onslaught than the heat-induced thirst of the Bajan skies. By then the score was 135 from 19 overs with Gilly on 95 from 66 balls and his silent partner, Haydos, on 30 from 49 balls.

There was little let-up from this incredible partnership until the fifth ball of the twenty-third over when Hayden was caught trying to hit Malinga over cover with the score on 172. Gilly was finally out five overs later having played one of the greatest innings of all the World Cups — 149 from 104 balls and his first 100 in World Cup competiton. What a time to produce it!! It was a personal triumph, just payment for the dedication, hard work and integrity in everything he had done throughout his cricket career.

The plunder continued and we were able to finish the shortened innings length of 38 overs at 5 for 281. An early wicket in Sri Lanka's chase and we were on our way. But Sanath Jayasuriya and Kumar Sangakkara had other ideas and their partnership had them well and truly in the game. However, just as the bowling group had done against any side that threatened in the tournament, they struck. This time, through the 'jack rabbit' Brad Hogg getting Sangakkara, and another seven wickets falling in the space of 12 overs, the game was ours (or so we thought). At this point, the Sri Lankan batsmen were offered the light which had been distinctly dark for some time, with still three overs left. From the players' perspective this was the end of the game and celebrations began.

In the coaches' area we were quite restrained as we had just been told that the full quota of overs had to be bowled, otherwise we would be trooping back the next day! Confusion reined. Fortunately, common sense prevailed with all parties agreeing to conclude the game in almost complete darkness.

It was time for all the players who had not been selected and the support staff to swoop onto the field and engulf the players who were inebriated on the sweetness of victory.

The end of match speeches and interviews seemed oddly long given the moon was already high in the sky — although speeches and interviews always seem long and an anticlimax at this juncture, whether you are the winning team that just want to celebrate or the losing team that just want to get off the oval as quickly as possible.

The champagne, the photos with the Cup, the lap of honour waving to an army of supporter groups who had travelled to Barbados for the finals, and the return to the dressing rooms where the stories flowed and the stuff that legends will be made from in years to come, were born.

'Underneath the Southern Cross I stand ...'

Mission complete, gentlemen!

18

Scouting the opposition

ONE OF THE BASIC features of every campaign is to do as much scouting of our opposition as possible. For the October 2006 ICC trophy we undertook significant profiling of each country in relation to their current player lists, involving vision of each player, how they were dismissed, how they scored their runs and how they bowled. We compiled this information in our computer system so we had an extremely comprehensive statistical and video analysis available for coaching staff and for our own players, which allowed us to formulate strategies. We continued to add to the profiles throughout the ICC Trophy and from other tournaments, so that the profiles would be comprehensive and up to date for the World Cup in 2007.

The scouting for the 2006-07 Ashes series was similar in that we compiled a visual, diagrammatic and statistics profile of the English team, but we also added some other useful reports to this base knowledge. I had spent the off-season (the English summer) researching media commentary of their team, especially when it emanated from within their ranks. I paid particular attention to comments made by their coach, Duncan Fletcher, Michael Vaughan, 'Freddie' Flintoff and Andrew Strauss, and there was some interesting reading from Kevin Pietersen, Ashley Giles and Monty Panesaar. Other anecdotal information came from Australian players who played county cricket in England, principally Shane Warne, Jason Gillespie and Darren Lehmann. In addition to this information a number of English players had published various books on the 2005 Ashes series which England had won. For me, Duncan Fletcher's diary, *Ashes Regained: the Coach's Story*, was a most useful handbook into their strategies, their dressing room thinking (or at least Fletcher's) and key moments during the series.

One of the important questions to answer is why do you need to spend time, energy, finance and personnel on the opposition, when these limited resources could be directed towards the improvement of your own team?

There are three major reasons why we seek to look inside our opposition. Firstly, it is about establishing *predictability* or *patterning.* That is, what are their players (batters and bowlers) more likely to do in certain game situations and, just as important, what strategies does the team use? My goal was to try to attain a 60 to 70 per cent correct assessment of the decision-making of an opposition. Without detailed examination, I believe we achieved around 70 per cent or better.

Secondly, if we are more aware of our opposition's *patterns of play,* then we can plan more precisely the delivery and execution of how we want to play the game. We can better determine what, where and when are the *match ups* that give us the most competitive advantage. Match ups is a term used to define a comparison of resources — personnel, financial, administrative, and so on. While a lot of information is in the minds of our players, built up from years of playing experience, we were able to complement this with additional data that showed which bowlers and bowling combinations would be most likely to create opportunities against a team, a player(s) or a set of conditions.

While this is standard practice for other sports like baseball, basketball and hockey, this supplementary detail is very new to cricket. In terms of 'taking the game to a new level' in statistical analysis of the game, and as a significant aid to onfield performance, the concept of match ups and the precision it adds to game tactics will be one avenue where those teams who understand how to best use the information will be well ahead of their opposition.

Thirdly, in looking more closely at our opposition, we may discover *techniques, skills* and *innovation* that we could use in our own preparation. The reverse of this approach has certainly occurred around the world as other teams have looked closely at what we have been doing. Other countries have imported many of our training techniques, contracted our coaching personnel and have used our facilities to try and close the gap between us and them.

The Australian Cricket Team have certainly looked at the creativity of batsmen from around the world. English county players, to some degree, have been at the forefront of creative techniques due to the amount of limited overs cricket played there. Indian, West Indian, Pakistani and Sri Lankan batsmen, who often do not have the strength and power of Australian players, have an incredible dexterity with their wrists.

From a bowling perspective, the actions of spin and pace bowlers from overseas countries have always been intriguing. Use of wrists, strength of fingers, different actions, getting the ball to swing violently — all of the individuals who demonstrate these skills have developed them with the express purpose of having something that no one else has. These unusual skills are designed to redress the dominance of bat over ball. Differences in technique need to be studied just as much as, and sometimes more than, traditional or 'correct' techniques.

It should also be realised that our opposition does not only come in the form of a person, team or organisation. It also comes in terms of the conditions that may prevail.

For example in India the temperatures are normally in the mid-to-high 30s. Places closer to the coastline, like Mumbai, also have very high humidity; the air feels coarse and is polluted. The people are fanatical about their cricket, constantly wanting to touch, photograph or chase a signature of the players they worship. Health is also an issue. There is always a bout of vomiting and diarrhoea lurking for the careless visitor. It is a case of continually being vigilant, understanding your body and what it needs, and having all the proper nutrition, fluids and medical support on hand.

Another key condition for us is the grounds, the training facilities, the dressing rooms and the type of wickets that we can expect to play on. In particular, the latter impacts directly on team strategy and the final squads and team selection.

The available training facilities often determine how much additional equipment we need to take with us to satisfy our preparation requirements. As part of this tour we had a bowling machine re-engineered so it could be made portable and taken with us for the entire trip. While each ground was to have a bowling machine made available to us, previous experience and our scouting reports of the West Indies led us to the correct conclusion that our own would be necessary as this would be a vital piece of our training equipment.

While we are unable to control all the external factors that threaten our ability to succeed, it is nonetheless worthwhile to acknowledge them. Even our financial resources directly impact on how we want to run the team and how professionally we can approach every aspect of performance.

How do we apply these observations and strategies to business?

As I mentioned earlier, *scouting the opposition* is only one of a suite of ingredients that go to make up a long standing successful team. Nevertheless, it is an important element. A business that does not pay due care and attention to the workings of its competitors provides fertile ground for takeover, loss of market share and an inability to compete for new markets.

A business needs to put appropriate resources into analysing the patterns and the predictability of key rivals. It needs to know how these competitors approach customers, acquisitions and deal with market conditions. In doing so, key areas which can give it competitive advantage can be clearly identified. Once identified, how to use this advantage, this 'match up' is the work of the organisational tacticians.

At the same time, good scouting will alert the business to special features, creative or innovative methods and other external environment benefits that can be used internally.

KEY MESSAGES

1. Ensure that analysis of your opposition is a key strategy in order to better predict their *patterns of play*.

2. Ensure appropriate and sufficient resources are devoted to analysis.

3. Search for areas of significant competitive advantage and match ups.

4. Be alert to innovations that can be quickly absorbed into your own business.

3. Ensure the analysis process factors in the current and the future environments that the team or business operates in.

19

Meeting the challenge

THIS SOMETHING I WROTE to the *Sunday Telegraph* (UK) before Australia played England in the Fifth Test, 2005. I have reproduced it here because it sums ups neatly the coaching principles I employed at the time when Australia was seen as the underdog.

'Life is not the way it is supposed to be. It is the way it is.
The way you cope with it is what makes the difference
(for you and those around you).'   INSTON HUR HI

The beauty and ecstasy, the doom and despair are all part of what is wrapped up in the tussle of international sport. Such extremes of emotion seem to have been a constant ingredient of the current 2005 Test series.

While similar emotions are felt for a range of reasons in everyday life, international sport condenses the extremities of normal living into a cauldron of tension, drama, patriotic fervour and exhilarating entertainment. All this occurs under the insatiable appetite of the public and the constant analyses of a voracious media.

With the roller coaster ride of being in front or behind comes the resultant challenges for player, team, support staff and coach.

From the coach's desk, the challenges are always present for the growth and development of an elite team — particularly one as successful as the Australian Cricket Team.

High on the list are:

- Maintaining the success rate of the team in both Test and one-day formats of the game.
- Managing the creation of change.
- managing our current and future playing resources.
- Ensuring all our support systems and processes are at the cutting edge of world's best practice.
- Keeping a clear eye on the future, in order to understand what it will take to move from the present and be in control of what lies ahead.

Like all coaches, managers and leaders of organisations, I operate from a set of principles — a coaching philosophy that gives me a framework from which to meet such challenges.

These principles can be explained as:

- **Vision** – I firmly believe in attempting to *control* the future by having playing skills and support technologies that no other team has, plus having the all-round skills to effectively react to whatever the future may throw at us.

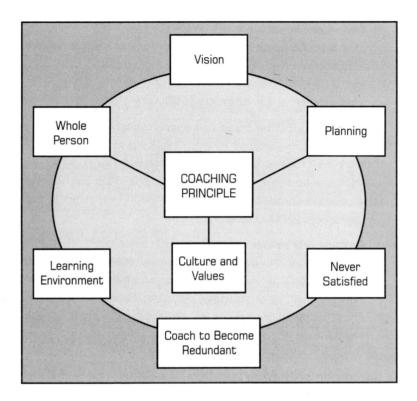

- **Create a learning environment** — Motivation comes from each individual, but it must be nurtured by a team environment which is challenging and encouraging of personal growth.

- **Never satisfied** — No matter how well or poorly we perform, results are only an outcome of a process of continually wanting to be better. Today is a benchmark for tomorrow.

- **Coach to be redundant** — If I do my job properly with each player, then I can retreat further and further from the individual. It is about them being totally responsible and accountable for their decisions and actions. Each player is to be a leader.

- **The whole person** — All of us involved with the production of a product for public consumption operate in the *people industry*. We happen to conduct our business in the sport sector of that industry. Nevertheless, I see the players with whom I work as people first and cricketers second.

- **Planning** — No business can operate successfully for any length of time without having a planning methodology. The planning process gives us a framework to work within — from the immediate needs of playing the Fifth Test, to the medium term needs of World Cup in 2007, and three to five years beyond this event.

- **Culture and values** — The *glue* which binds these principles together are the intangible elements often posted in the organisation's orientation booklet, and includes words or phrases such as punctuality, discipline, honesty, hard work, trust, respect and tradition. Whatever the mantra, the words must actually be *lived*, not just be platitudes.

So, how does this set of principles help define what is required to be done for the remaining Test of the series?

I believe it helps:

- Define our key issues and priorities for the immediate term (Fifth Test) and the future.

- Identify what we need to analyse and the relevant solutions.

- Clearly outline the practicalities of these solutions in relation to 'having all the team on the same page'.

Obviously I am not about to provide England with any great insight to our preparations for the remaining Test, but let me outline some of the thinking and the planning (not in any order of priority) that has and will be undertaken in the build up to the final showdown.

This Australian cricket team has not been subject to such competitive scrutiny since the series in India in 2001 and the series against New Zealand in Australia at the end of 2001. Before and after these two series Australia seemed unbeatable, as indeed this current team has been until this tour.

As a result, criticism has grown in magnitude and ferocity with every passing day of the tour. Teams in such situations can feel that they are under siege. While other teams are subject to this constant inspection too, such a non-stop barrage over so many aspects of on-field performance and off-field activities is foreign to this Australian team.

So, it is essential for the coach to make sure he sticks to his guiding principles and is consistent in their application.

The coach needs to keep a clear head and keep his emotions under control, so he can decide on and deal with the real issues and not be consumed by the ever present *bushfires* that are simply outside his control.

For example, we have had a problem with the number of no-balls our quick bowlers are delivering. As a team we have a *zero tolerance* policy on no-balls, it's one of the measures we have agreed on as an indicator of overall bowling performance — it's not something that I, as the coach, have pulled out of thin air in the hope that the problem will be fixed.

So, what is the issue?

Firstly, there is no argument that it needs to be fixed quickly as it affects our on-field momentum. We've taken at least eight English wickets only to be denied by the plaintive cry of 'no-ball' from the umpire. It is also interesting to note that England has bowled approximately the same number, but as they are performing better than we are, then it is not perceived, at least publicly, as a problem.

So the 'no-ball bushfire' has been the source of much media attention; experts calling for bowling coaches, new training methods, a different coaching regime, and internally there have been a range of suggestions to 'put out the fire'. All have varying degrees of merit and some have been factored into our training, with limited success.

However, I believe the key issue which will have greater longer term affect is the answer to the question: *What standards (performance, training, preparation, behaviour, team culture) are we prepared to accept?*

We discussed these standards before we left home shores, but it is obvious we all need to revisit them to ensure we establish appropriate standards, and then, more importantly, set about meeting them.

As Jack Welch, the former CEO of General Electric said:

'We now know where productivity – real and limitless productivity — comes from. It comes from challenged, empowered, excited, rewarded teams of people.'

The coach must work with the players to deal with these immediate needs, but always be clear about the real issue and where the long term solutions lie.

It has been argued throughout this series that the primary reason for Australia not playing to its abilities has been due to the way England have played. If this is the case, how can we change that situation for the fifth Test?

There is no doubt over the last three–five years change has been occurring in the England set-up which has culminated in how they are playing now.

As with any business that aims to be number one in its industry sector, it scans the horizon for *best practice*. Where possible it copies the practices, systems and processes of the industry leader. Another strategy is to import expertise to accelerate change.

The England and Wales Cricket Board must be given great credit for looking at what Australian cricket has been doing. It has been proactive, importing national coaches in John Harmer and Rod Marsh to significantly improve coach education and the English cricket academy.

Further, the Board has:

- Supported the structure and vision of Duncan Fletcher.
- Provided resources for the national team.
- Supported the implementation of a central contract system.

- Stabilised the selection process through better talent identification.

- Assisted in the improvement of a team culture as opposed to a culture based on individualism.

So, back to the fundamental question: given these advances in English cricket, how then are we going to turn the tide in such a short time? How is this so-called aging and under-performing Australian team going to upset the favourites, England?

It is as simple and complex as playing with 'freedom' — that is — playing with typical Australian spirit, Australian passion and Australian skills.

We have seen most of this type of play in the fourth innings of each game. The simple game plan is to reproduce this standard for the whole of this final game of the Ashes tour.

It's amazing this fourteen week tour has come down to the very last game. As it has unfolded, all the games that have gone before were simply the preliminary rounds. We now have the only game that counts in the series, the Fifth Test at the Oval — the season's 'grand final'.

I could not conclude this without a quote from the master tactician, Sun Tzu, in *The Art of War:*

He will win who knows when to fight and when not to fight. He will win who knows how to handle both superior and inferior forces. He will win whose army is animated by the same spirit throughout all its ranks. He will win who, prepared himself, waits to take the enemy unprepared.

20

Taking the game to a new level

AT THE PRESS CONFERENCE immediately following our win in the 2003 World Cup I was asked the question, 'How much can this side improve now that it has taken the game to a new level — what is there left to achieve?'

My reply was simple and unambiguous: 'We can improve a lot across all areas of our cricket because I do not believe we have taken the game to a new level. I believe we play the same way as all other teams, utilising similar basic skills. The difference is that we deliver these skills better and more consistently than other teams. And we are very fortunate that we have players who are already regarded as greats of the game to help with the delivery of these skills.'

However, the fact remains, that to take the game to a new level requires us to rethink all our technical, physical, tactical and mental skills to ascertain what can be done differently, more effectively within reasonable boundaries of time and resources. It is my contention that in the whole history of cricket only three people have changed the game: England captain Douglas Jardine's bodyline bowling (also known as leg-theory); West Indian captain Clive Lloyd's quartet of fast bowlers; and Australian media magnate Kerry Packer's World Series Cricket revolution. These men introduced a concept that no one else had ever thought to do, and made it work.

Various individuals like Sir Donald Bradman (batting), Shane Warne (leg-spin bowling) and Glenn McGrath (fast bowling) have made an impact on the game in setting new benchmarks. So did Steve Waugh's aggressive win or lose, no draws approach — through increasing the runs scored per over and higher totals per day, and taking wickets through attacking longer.

But how can you take the game to another level?

For me, the process had its origins in a lecture I attended in Brisbane in the late 1980s. It was given by Dr Edward de Bono and called *The Process of Thinking* in which Edward proceeded to enthral the audience with his theories and examples of how to think differently, or as he termed it, **laterally**.

For a period of some three hours he took us on a journey that demonstrated how our thinking is constrained by history. Therefore in order to solve problems he has devised a range of strategies to challenge conventional approaches.

Indeed, Steve Waugh and I visited him during the 2001 Ashes tour to discuss some of his ideas. From this brief meeting I was able to invite him to meet with a small group of players and administrators during the following domestic season in Sydney.

•

These encounters encouraged me to constantly question the status quo. I am certainly not skilled in Edward de Bono's techniques, but I subscribe totally to his process. Rather than 'if it ain't broke, don't fix it', de Bono's theory is 'if it ain't broke, break it!'

There's a methodology to which many organisations and particularly sporting organisations adhere which I term the **Fred Flintstone principle**.

The principle goes, why would Fred want to change anything, when he can drive to work everyday in his *flow-through air-conditioned* car with its puncture-proof stone wheels and then return to his stone home and enjoy a brontosaurus steak cooked by his loving wife, Wilma? Why would he want to change?

Everything works; Fred is satisfied!

There is a certainty with life, a kind of 'comatose complacency'. Due to the lack of ambition or, in an organisation's case, its presiding culture, an ever-increasing decline begins.

That is why I believe we must question everything we do. Not only the things that aren't working, but also things that are. We must constantly seek ways of improving what we do — **keep raising the bar**.

As a coach, I believe I would not be doing my job effectively if I wasn't constantly seeking ways to improve everything we do, constantly trying to challenge players and take them to heights they've never been to before.

So when asked if we can improve, the answer is 'yes'!

In preparation for our assault on the 2007 World Cup, I wanted to improve our playing skills, especially our fielding, as this is a major defensive aspect of one-day cricket, and I believed that the team with the best defence would win the trophy. So I employed a baseball coach, Mike Young, who I had worked with at Queensland Cricket and introduced to the Australian team just prior to the 2003 World Cup.

He is an excellent skills coach, but also an excellent coach generally speaking. That is to say, Mike knows how to work with people, particularly athletes. So for me, he brought not only new skills and drills to improve our on-field performance, but also a new culture — a different dynamic which was important through the course of a long campaign.

Prior to the World Cup Final I used a quote from the legendary Chinese warlord, Sun Tzu who said, 'Invincibility comes from defence; attack gives you the opportunity for success.' Mike's work, together with our planning strategies and the players' skills, gave us additional confidence in our ability to contain teams with the ball and defend totals. And as history now shows, our attack through our top four batsmen gave us the opportunity for success. It was then left to our defence to seal the title of World Cup Champions.

So, way back, straight after the post-match press conference when I was asked whether the side could improve, I began considering a range of strategies for the following four years in preparation for the 2007 World Cup:

1. Increasing the influence of baseball **throwing techniques**.

2. Adapting baseball-style approaches to **tactical signalling** throughout play.

3. By developing **multi-dimensional players**, that is players who are skilled on both sides of their bodies (left-handed and right-handed), it's as though we increase the number of players we have on the field — metaphorically speaking, more than 11 players in the field and more than two batsmen at the crease.

4. Coaching world's best practice means adopting **the best of the best**. Each of the game's great players has unique technical and mental attributes that set them apart from the rest. We needed to analyse and harness these skills and traits within the coaching and development of future players.

5. Linked to this 'best of the best' and 'world's best practice' is **research**. Challenge the basic theories and 'rules' of coaching and contemporary understanding of the game. For example, cricket fitness — what is it?

6. **Technology** is now commonplace for most international and first class teams — investigate how technology can be more effectively used to gain advantage.

7. **Statistical analysis** of the game should provide us with more precise patterns of oppositions in order to enhance our tactical preparation.

8. **Skills training practices** needed to be enhanced and made more professional.

It was time not to be Fred Flintstone!

To achieve these goals required us all to think laterally about our cricket — myself, the other coaches, players, selectors, support staff and administrators. We had to think laterally about the way it is played, the way it could be played, the athletes that would be required to play that way, and the skills matrix those athletes would need to have.

I cannot for one moment say that we achieved all of these goals before or during the 2007 World Cup. But I believe that the team, and all those associated with the team, benefited from striving to change the game and take it to a new level.

Hopefully, the footprints are clear and the teams, players and staff who follow will continue to raise that bar.

At my last press conference in Barbados after we had won the World Cup for the third consecutive occasion, I was again asked about the team's performance: 'Three World Cups, undefeated in its last 29 matches, some incredible individual performers and performances — how now do you describe this team?'

My answer: '**They are the perfect team because each day they want to improve and take the game to a new level!**'

KEY MESSAGES

1. Do not assume the current way is the best way or the only way — constantly seek others.

2. Use a range of devices at your disposal to search out other ways, such as questioning, lateral thinking, outside experiences, research, technology, the internet and so on.

21

Professionalism

SCANNING THE BUSINESS AND sports pages of the daily newspapers, readers' attention is often drawn to the high salaries of business executives and our sporting elite. Many people ask: 'Why are these people paid so much? Can the company or the game really afford it? Is anybody worth that amount of money? Why should they be paid more than the Prime Minister?

Before we can answer these questions, there are two more fundamental questions that needs to be answered. 'What do we understand by the term 'professional?' and 'Are our top executives and our sports stars actually our leading professionals?'

To answer these questions, the first point that needs clarification is monetary payment. Simply because one is paid for services does not guarantee professionalism. Conversely, because one is not paid, does not mean they cannot be professional. For example, in people who act as volunteers — for charity, junior sport, service organisations or a parent running a household — I see complete dedication to the task, not only to its completion, but completion to the highest possible standards.

That's professionalism without pay. On the other hand, I see some highly paid sporting personalities who, on many fronts, pay lip service to what being a true professional means.

The Australian Cricket Team, a highly motivated, highly skilled and highly successful team of athletes, verges on professionalism to varying degrees. Like another sporting code, Rugby Union, cricket is still coming to grips with what professionalism means for the sport.

In my role of coach, I would see outstanding examples of **professionalism** from all players within the Australian team every day. I recall a pre-match preparation session with Matthew Hayden in Cairns. We were playing Sri Lanka and Matthew wanted to have his game in the best shape possible to counter the Sri Lankan attack. We spent an hour on the bowling machine where for the first twenty minutes he did not hit one ball — he just watched the line and length around his off stump. For the next twenty minutes he moved more into the line of the ball and selectively played at it. For the final twenty minutes he proceeded to play a range of shots. The essence of this session was to create a **clear decision-making process** for what shots he would and would not play against the opposition.

Another more recent case was during the off-season leading into the 2006-07 season. As coaching staff we would provide all players with a physical and technical program tailored to their specific needs. Michael Hussey wrote back accepting our views, but he had incorporated them into a three-page dossier of exactly what he would be doing, when and how it was going to be achieved.

Another example was Justin 'Alfie' Langer who had returned home early from the South Africa-Bangladesh tour due to the very heavy blow to the head from the South African opening bowler, Machaya Ntini. He trained the house down at home through April, May and June and was as fit as a bull. Most importantly, though, it was the time he was able to devote to his wife and young family that provided him the perfect balance. However, he knew he had to get back in the middle again — he needed to know where his cricket was. He sacrificed his family time and the comforts of home to accept a short-tenure county cricket contract to test his skills, his mental game, his desire, his attitude and his commitment. The outcome was successful, because of Alfie's professional approach to his sport.

The stars of the Australian Cricket Team, or any sporting team, are all professionals because they 'know their game'. They know their skills and how to deliver them, plus they know the game itself — what it is, what it takes to be constantly successful and where the game is going.

As a consequence, the long-term star performers who generally become regarded as 'greats' of the game are always looking at ways to improve. There was a quote made about Roger Federer after he'd won Wimbledon in 2006 that truly reflects this type of professional attitude: 'It's not how good he is, it is about how good he can be'.

Wayne Gretsky, the great ice hockey player, number 99 for the Edmonton Oilers, was once quoted as saying: 'I don't skate to where the puck is, I skate to where it will be.' While his statement can apply to game time — his anticipation of the play enabling him to be in the right place at the right time — I have no doubt that the meaning behind it is that for him to continue to be the best, he had to read where the game was going and train to get there before anyone else.

Great players never give up or give in. Whether it's an injury, performance slump, not meeting the expectations of themselves and others, or off-field distractions, they have the capacity to deal with these issues so they are able to get back onto the stage where they are the star.

I think most of the Australian Cricket Team players are further advanced along the *professionalism continuum* than the support environment around them, such as the coaches, medical and paramedical people, fitness staff, administrators, facilities managers and so on. In cricket, the people who occupy those support positions have generally learnt their skills and trade from within the sport itself. And while the support structure needs to have a very good 'feel' for the game, cricket is still too traditional, too hierarchical and too inward looking to comprehend what truly professional sport demands.

Like any other sport, Cricket Australia has to cope with an internal conflict in its delivery and administration. On the one hand, it must promote its financial lifeblood, the competitive aspect of sport, the flagship of which is the Australian Cricket Team. While Tests and One-Day Internationals generate the majority of revenue for the sport, they are also costly to run. Significant expenditures such as player salaries, travel and accommodation around the world, conducting national competitions and running the Centre of Excellence program all draw heavily on revenue.

In addition, Cricket Australia must promote the development of the game. This is really about the attraction to, and retention of, people — junior cricketers, girls and boys, be they city or country cricketers, volunteers and officials who help run the game at club and community level, and spectators who have a range of expectations that need to be satisfied.

Partly as a result of this dual delivery, the support structures and environment around the Australian Cricket Team can only be considered as semi-professional. That is to say, it cannot deliver a total dedication of commitment and, more importantly, resources to the standards demanded by a fully professional national team.

However, these are the strategic choices that Cricket Australia has to make in terms of growing its business. Does it choose the competition side with the national team as its beacon? Does it choose the development side with grass roots cricket as its driver? Or does it continue with the current strategy of doing both?

In a global context, Australian cricket is still seen to be the leader. But as other countries gradually understand what this new era of professionalism means (i.e. that producing a national team which is highly successful for an extended period requires a large investment) Australia's tenure as top dog becomes increasingly at risk.

KEY MESSAGES

1. Professionalism is about standards and commitment, not about being paid or unpaid.

2. Professionalism is about 'knowing your game' and what is required to deliver that 'game'.

3. Professionalism is also about total dedication to being the best, and never giving in.

4. Professionalism can involve personal sacrifices.

5. Professionalism is about understanding where the 'game' is going and being prepared to get there before anyone else.

6. To be professional requires a significant investment in all support structures and systems.

7. A sport or business needs to clearly understand the consequences of the strategic choices it makes in pursuit of, or non-pursuit of, professionalism.

22

Your strength is your weakness

IT WAS TUESDAY, 13 March 2001, the third day of the Second Test against India at the Eden Gardens in Kolkata. We had won the First Test convincingly and had India on the ropes. The tour had been dubbed Steve Waugh's 'final frontier' as he had yet to win a tour in India. We had won fifteen Tests in a row until then, a world record. We were seen as unstoppable due to our aggressive game: scoring runs at an incredible rate for Test cricket, and playing with attacking fields to quality bowling, missing few opportunities that came our way. It didn't seem to matter whether we batted or bowled first, where we played or what situation we found ourselves in, this Australian team could not be beaten.

So with a seemingly unbeatable first innings lead of 274, the moment arrived for Stephen Roger Waugh to decide whether to enforce the follow-on or take the safety route which would be to bat again. The latter decision would have taken India totally out of the game and their best result could only be a draw. But there was little hesitation in the Australian dressing rooms: we should continue to do what we had been doing so successfully

— be aggressive, dominate and bury the opposition. So the follow-on was enforced.

In the end, however, that decision did not favour us. There were some factors outside our control which conspired against us, such as India changing their batting order which allowed VVS Laxman to open after being 50 odd not out in the first innings, some dubious umpiring decisions, a rampant and highly charged Eden Gardens stadium, incessant heat, and ultimately two players, Laxman and Rahul Dravid, who played possibly the best innings of their careers.

For all that though, the biggest factor that finally brought the Australian team to its knees and this incredible winning sequence to an end was the team itself. We continued to play our brand of cricket. We were on the verge of making more history. The winning record would have been increased and we would have achieved the first Test series win in India since Bill Lawry's team in 1969.

We were almost eyeballing the result. However, we became blinded by the endpoint rather than working out how to get there. We believed that provided we kept playing to our strengths finally something would break our way — lady luck would turn. There were no fallback options, no Plan B or Plan C.

We were faced with two players demonstrating that they could withstand, counter and then attack the Australian cricket machine. It was inconceivable, at least inconceivable for the length of time Dravid and Laxman repelled Australia and turned the whole momentum of the Test match, and ultimately the series, around. One of the hallmarks of this Australian team was that there was always a player or players who would put their hand up with a special performance that would allow us to gain or regain control of a game. Now the boot was well and truly on the other foot and we had little or no defence – *our strength had become our weakness.*

For fifteen Test matches our approach had served us very well. On this occasion, though, we needed more than an individual piece of brilliance. We needed more than lady luck to deliver us a couple of umpiring verdicts. We needed some defensive planning, some patience to deliver those plans and less emotional distractions from making good quality decisions. But this was not part of our 'war plan' — the best means of defence had been 'attack'. As a consequence, the players were becoming increasingly tired, frustrated and emotional about what was happening (or indeed, not happening).

The series was one all with one to play. And India's momentum, its confidence, and the fanatical support to the team was massive. In the final session of the game we had the opportunity to salvage a draw. However, by this time, the team had been physically drained. More importantly, it had been mentally drained so that the mindset and strategies to fight out a draw were also not in place. We lost the so-called 'unloseable' test.

One often sees similar occurrences with organisations which are having enormous success due to particular strategies. Their attitude is while things are working successfully, why change? The old adage 'if it ain't broke, don't fix it' was coined for a reason. It seems, too, that we can become superstitious: that is to say, provided we keep doing exactly the same, not changing any routines, then we will continue to be successful.

There is no doubt that what brings us success needs to be clearly understood because if we can repeat these steps, mechanisms, strategies and decisions, we give ourselves the best chance of repeating success. However, in understanding the means to success it is obvious that there are many events and circumstances outside our control, which have the capacity to impact adversely on us achieving the desired results.

Consequently, there is a need to build into a formula for success a range of 'fall back' options and strategies that will help counter obstacles to continuing success.

Some of these fall back options include:

- The ability to recognise when proven methods are potentially under threat.

- The ability to remain objective in analysing performance, so that decision-making is not blinded by loyalty to the proven success formula.

- Being fully appreciative of all your personal resources — staff, energy and negative changes in internal environment — to ensure you have what's needed to maintain your success.

- Never underestimating the capacity of human endeavour to achieve great deeds.

We all want to continually play to our strengths — in sport, in business and in life. However, to think that our strengths will always overcome or be greater than our competitors is poor planning and poor leadership. Achilles, the Greek warrior, fatally believed his great fighting ability would always be his saviour.

Understand your strengths and use them as often as possible. But also understand that to have them as your only means leaves you vulnerable to defeat.

KEY MESSAGES

1. Know clearly what your strengths are.

2. Identify quickly when these strengths are not the appropriate strategies for the prevailing circumstances.

3. Ensure you have 'fall back' options for those times when your strengths are not working.

23

And how is your day, anyway?

AFTER BEING ON THE road with the Australian team for some time, it is always great to get home, get back into normal family routines and sleep in your own bed!

While you're away from home plenty of jobs build up that need attending to and they wait like little booby-traps. I stumbled across one of these the other day as I sat down at the computer and tried to use the local network we have set up. Networking allows an increasing number of family computer users to have relatively good access for most computer needs.

There was a connection problem with the network and, like all good human beings, the family had adapted to the prevailing conditions. Hence no one had bothered to send for help from our computer support person.

So I rang John, our computer man, on his mobile. I hadn't spoken with him since well before I had left for the various series we'd played in and outside Australia. Possibly the last conversation we'd had had been about six months before, and about some technology hiccup.

And how is your day, anyway?

John answered the phone and I asked whether I could trouble him for five minutes to which he replied yes, although he was working with another customer at the time. In the background I could hear music and inquired what the 'noise' was, to which he replied that it was his other mobile with a call from another customer. They would have to wait, he said.

I blurted out what I perceived to be the problem, to which he directed me through a cascade of icons, properties, tabs, ticked boxes and a return to the main menu to see if he had solved the glitch — it hadn't.

At this point John interrupted his over-the-phone-support service and asked, 'And how is your day anyway?'

In those few words he caught me totally off guard! I hadn't rung this guy for six months and the last time I talked to him (and it was most likely at him, not with him) was about some minor breakdown that had once again needed immediate attention.

So here I was, not ringing and saying 'G'day, John, how are you? How's the business? Can you call me back when it is convenient for you?' Instead, I was just bowling ahead because I thought my need was the most important need in the world at that moment in time, regardless of others.

We stopped the previous one-way communication, enjoyed an exchange of pleasantries, agreed that he had a little bit of time to help me, and then discussed what else may be required. It was a satisfying outcome for both of us.

That little episode, brought home a couple of very important messages to me about our everyday interactions with people.

And these simple human interactions are important factors for being a good coach.

The first of these is a clear recognition that while you may have an issue that, in your opinion, requires immediate attention, other people around you are often *not* in a convenient position to help you. So, your call for assistance should always be prefaced with some real interest expressed in the other's current circumstances. To do this effectively, one must be *in the moment*, not distracted by personal thoughts and needs.

The second, which is part of the first, is to catch the person doing the right thing! How often when we converse with peers, staff, children, students or athletes do we confront them with things they have done wrong? Very rarely do we contact someone on the basis of *praise first*.

Overlooking the good things is a trap I have sometimes fallen into with our Australian cricketers. Not just with the younger players, but also the older players. Putting my needs before others and overlooking the good as opposed to the bad are both cardinal sins of coaching.

Part of the reason (and I'm not for one moment excusing it) is having been so closely associated with the Australian team for a good number of years. For example, I've been guilty of making assumptions on the transition process of new players from State cricket into the Australian team. Some do it very easily, others take time to adjust. But those initial phases are crucial to the personal development and retention of that player. Trying to perform on the international stage is difficult at the best of times, let alone when a player, or a new support staff member, are trying to do it first up.

Brett Dorey was a case in point. The big, lanky fast bowler from Western Australia was a surprise selection into the Australian One-Day International team in early 2006. He was an older lad, twenty-six years old, and arrived with an air of confidence and maturity. He trained well and had a few Western Australian team-mates to welcome him into the group. However, after being selected for a match against Sri Lanka in Sydney, his onfield performance was well below expectation — his and ours!

From that point forward he was a changed person — unsure of himself, a little withdrawn, angry, frustrated, and didn't know exactly where to turn. Fortunately, a conversation with Mike Hussey (our Mr Fixit, our anchorman) helped and then I realised what had happened and how I had failed him. Basically, I had assumed he would be one of those players who would fit seamlessly into the team and was more than ready to be given a chance in competition. However, although Brett appeared confident I hadn't checked how he was really feeling and didn't realise he needed some assistance with his transition.

Fortunately, the story had a reasonably happy ending. Brett returned to his home state, regained his feet and the national selectors rewarded him with selection to the winter Commonwealth Bank Academy program, where he has been improving his training, preparations and on-field performance under the tutelage of our national coaches.

In terms of the older players — the tried, tested and well performed — such as Ponting, Hayden, Langer, Martyn, McGrath, Lee, Warne, Kasprowicz, Gillespie and MacGill, one takes for granted what they do, game in, game out. The consequence of this is an expectation of what they should do individually and, therefore, what the team should do collectively, because of their influence. The bar is set ever higher, and not being able to jump this bar (probably nine out of ten times) becomes a somewhat disappointing result.

Because of my long-term experience as a coach with Queensland and Australia, I tend to take more gulps of coaching formula from the half-empty glass as my time with a player increases than I do in the initial stages where I drink mainly from the half-full. This means I start off with a positive perspective — an approach that is not based on expectation, but one based on being *in the moment* with the individual as much as I can. But as time goes on and my expectations of the person grow, I can neglect praise for the many good things they are doing.

Obviously, good coaching requires a bit of both. But the important thing is to tailor your approach for the individual and the situation — the coach should consider *how, when, with whom* and *for what purpose* when delivering his cards. If continual improvement is part of the team culture (and it should be part of every team's culture regardless of how successful the team is) then it is about getting the balance, the proper fit for the current circumstances and players — that is the art of coaching.

KEY MESSAGES

1. Always be in the moment, and give full attention to the person with whom you are talking.

2. Recognise people for the good things they do rather than the negative.

3. Take the half-full, positive approach rather than the half-empty, negative one.

4. Do not assume or take for granted how people feel — find out!

24

Communication

'COMMUNICATION' IS AN EXTREMELY vague term that can be boiled down to two very basic constructs: what message do you wish to send (communicate); and am I able to 'hear' (receive) the message?

Most of us would have undertaken a simple exercise in communication (or the lack of it) in some form, like the group training program called Chinese Whispers. The essence is that a message is created at one point of a circle of people and passed from one to another until it returns back to the originator. Depending on the number of intermediaries, the message that comes back to the originator is significantly changed from what was said in the first place. Why does this occur in what would seem to be a very simple exercise? In my opinion it occurs because the sender has not clearly delivered the message to the receiver who, in turn, has not properly heard the message. The receiver has not given full (100 per cent) attention to receiving the message, or has been unable to receive or remember some of the message due to its quantity or quality. This could be due to a number of things including tone, language and the surroundings.

Communication is such a broad, all encompassing term that it means different things to different people. We need to think about communication problems in three ways so they can be fixed — either they're a sending problem, a receiving problem, or combination of both.

Communication is a crucial element of good coaching. Quite often it is something I find difficult to achieve. No matter how well I know a player or staff member — and this often dictates the timing and the way in which the message is delivered — I either ignore or overlook the best way of doing it. Obviously, this can lead to confusion and conflict, and time and energy is needed to reshape and re-deliver a message.

As an example, we had an interesting issue with our bowling group, as all cricket teams do. The issue was about the players not bowling no-balls in games. It is one of the few easily quantifiable measures of whether a player is doing something right or wrong. It is much more about process than outcomes such as taking a wicket or not, taking a catch or not and scoring runs or not. Hence, for a professional athlete, it should be straightforward, that to bowl a no-ball is unacceptable. Unfortunately, the bowling fraternity, while aware that it does provide the opposition with additional run scoring chances and sometimes denies a bowler a wicket, allow themselves to bowl a small percentage.

At training, the percentage of no-balls bowled is far worse, especially when the bowler affords himself the luxury mind-set of 'training is about rhythm'. So, at training the front foot line is of secondary importance.

Along with coaching staff and the batting group, I have attempted over and over again to make 'train as you play' the key message. As a consequence, there should be zero tolerance on no-balls at training. We wanted the bowlers to understand this message — which I believe they do — but I also wanted them to wear the responsibility of doing it ... all the time.

In the DLF Cup in Malaysia in September 2006, the bowling group decided that they would have 'our front foot there and thereabouts' for training. This response was totally inadequate because they had provided themselves with an escape route. But because we had given the bowlers the ownership to solve the problem, it was accepted by the group. By the end of the tournament, we had not only bowled an excessive number of no-balls, but also, in my opinion, the bowling group had demonstrated their inability to listen to the message and solve the problem.

A few weeks later, at the team meeting for the beginning of the ICC Trophy in India, I outlined our strategy for this tournament. The strategy was outlined in a document which was our framework, our map for playing all our one-day cricket through to and including the 2007 World Cup. In the meeting, we effectively agreed on its contents. The only topic of concern was the issue of not bowling any no-balls, which raised the ire of some bowlers. However, the message was conveyed clearly and agreed as a set of standards that the Australian Cricket Team would adhere to until the end of the World Cup.

After the first game, I found myself embroiled in an argument with Brett Lee about how this had interfered with his bowling by making him concentrate on not bowling no-balls, rather than just bowling. In part, he was correct. On game day, Brett needs to be able to go out and bowl fast with no technical issue in his mind. When his mind is clear, he can then make on-field tactical decisions based on team game plans and current circumstances. For him to be concerned where his front foot lands is the last thing he needs. But all of this should be taken care of at training. Training provides the constant and consistent repetition (the 'muscle memory') to allow game day to be automatic.

For Brett, and indeed, for most of our bowlers, herein lies the basic problem. The bowlers were not prepared to 'train as you play' — they didn't concentrate on getting the front foot behind the line to reinforce the 'muscle memory' system. They were not prepared to be totally accountable, totally professional in their bowling preparation for games.

Admittedly, during training the bowlers often felt the wrath of other members of the team, as the no-ball line is one of the few easily visible errors. A poor shot batting, a poor throw fielding or a dropped catch, often fall into categories of acceptable margins for error. In addition, the facilities for bowlers are often sub-standard compared with that of their batting counterparts.

But the no-balls at training phenomenon is not something which is required only when they reach the national team. It has been something that those bowlers would have practised probably since they were fifteen or sixteen years old and was eliminated then. Fundamentally, players must understand the concept of 'train as you play'. It is how the message is conveyed and then how it is received that will ultimately determine problems like the eradication of no-balls at training, and have an ultimate flow on effect on game day. At the same time, coaches need to be open to receiving the bowler's messages when situations and facilities will not permit a 'train as you play' environment.

Provided there is a willingness to receive messages that are sent and a willingness to actively deal with these messages, 'communication breakdown', the perennial communication problem, should be minimised.

KEY MESSAGES

1. Understand clearly the concept that is being relayed.

2. Know your target audience, group or individual so the concept can be delivered in messages that are easily understood.

3. Check formally and informally that the messages conveyed have been heard, understood and enacted.

4. If there is a 'lack of communication', find the specific problem(s) — they will be in the sending, the receiving, or a combination.

5. Constantly review the sending and receiving of messages.

25

It's in the stars

IAN 'HEALS' HEALY, THE former Australian record-breaking wicketkeeper, tells a humorous story about his team-mate, Shane Warne. It is a fictional story, but it is laced with enough hints of truth to give an insight to the man who has made Number 23 famous on the world stage of international cricket.

Healy and Shane were in the West Indies one morning when Warney came down to breakfast — which in itself is our first lead that the story is based more on fiction than fact — and announced that thirty-eight pairs of socks have been stolen from the fifty pairs he brought with him.

This immediately sends everyone into a fluster of concern and inquiry... except Healy. Instead Heals sat there and analysed what Warney had said and, after due consideration, alerted everyone to what had actually transpired.

He turned to Warney and said, 'Mate, you know you always exaggerate about what you say you have. In fact, you basically double your possessions. So, you didn't begin the tour with fifty pairs of socks, it was actually only twenty-five pairs. Next, I know you. To indicate you have only twelve pairs of socks left, you really have twenty-four pairs left, because you like to increase the drama and attention by at least fifty per cent.'

'So actually, mate, the truth of the story is, you brought twenty-five pairs of socks. You still have twenty-four in your possession. So we are talking about *one* pair of socks that have gone missing! And I am sure we will find them in your room somewhere...'

While this story is basically fictional, it gives some insights into *star performers* (celebrities) and their make-up.

I think there are three types of star performers. The first are *shooting stars* who burn brightly for a brief period, but do not have an understanding that talent is only one dimension of long-term performance. Talent must be nurtured, developed and applied for a long period of time to achieve long-lasting success.

We generally see such athletes in the junior ranks. How many outstanding juniors do you remember and where are they now? Where are the stars of your school teams or junior representative teams? Basically, these young stars have never been made aware of the talents they possess. Whether it's the environment in which they grow up, the lack of coaching and guidance they receive from their elders, whether they can't commit to the rigours of harnessing their talent, or (most likely) some combination of these, whatever the mix we all shake our heads at the terrrible waste of God-given talent.

It's in the stars

The next group are the *Halley's Comets*. We see their stardom every so often. They can perform outstandingly, better than all their peers, but then they fade, only to return intermittently. Their returns are marked by a gradual lessening of their brightness. My view of this group is that there is an innate mental flaw in their make-up. Deep down these individuals do not believe in themselves, and every time their brightness dims it merely serves to reinforce what seems to be a deeply rooted lack of belief in themselves.

Finally, there are those who continue to shine like the *Southern Cross*. They are the benchmark, forever shining, always there when you need them, reliable and enigmatic.

Do we need stars? Of course we do! They are the magicians of their craft. They do things that even their peers marvel at. Put simply, they do the actual business of winning games, or at least significantly influencing the final result, while delivering the show business (entertainment) at the same time.

So how do we encourage and manage stars? How do we deal with them?

As coach of a national team and a parent of five children, my view is that we need to place great emphasis on addressing their early years of stardom. The talented young athlete needs balance in their life, a very good understanding of right and wrong, and an understanding that there are always consequences for their actions, good or bad.

I don't believe in specialisation in summer and winter sports until as late as possible in the physical and mental development of the child. Furthermore, I do not believe in specialisation within the sports in which they are involved. Children need the broadest possible exposure to a range of physical activities and the different regulations and socialising processes that occur within each sport. Parents should avoid for as long as possible having their 'star' son or daughter placed on the conveyor belt of representative teams. Bear in mind, no matter in which setting these children are placed they will always shine! Equally, the coaches and managers of these players need to ensure the 'star' receives the appropriate skill training for their stage of development. Often because they are stars, the athlete is overlooked because they dominate on the sports field anyway.

In a perfect world as head coach of a national sporting team, I know that my star performers have been through the best development system. They understand their talents, know how to apply those talents and look for new challenges to enhance their talents. They take personal responsibility for everything they do, they have a clear picture on what comes with being a star and the associated highs and pitfalls, and they are fully aware of the needs of all those around them, while not neglecting themselves. What a dream!

How, then, did I manage the stars within the Australian Cricket Team?

There is certainly no one recipe that fits all. But there are some basic approaches which I tried to adopt.

The first and most important approach was to establish a relationship. But relationships vary because everyone is different.

The stars in our team had varying degrees of responsibility and accountability for their actions, a range of other people in their lives who would significantly influence their decision making, and they came from various backgrounds so, consequently, their opinions varied on how the coach could help them. I found our relationship depended on how much the star wanted the coach to get to know them. However, regardless of the amount, I would always keep the door open for them.

Warney was very much a case in point. He and I have different backgrounds and dissimilar views on various matters. This is not necessarily a bad thing — in fact, I believe it only enhances the development of a team and individuals within teams if some 'healthy' conflict exists. Our relationship was not 'best buddy' status. Neither of us would just ring up to ask 'How are you going?' or drop in to each other's room on tour to talk about life or the game. I think we both understood that. However, I have a huge amount of respect for what Warney has done for cricket and to be around one of the game's greatest ever players was a privilege. At the same time, I continually shook my head at some of the other things that occurred in Warney's life.

For instance, the diuretic drugs debacle immediately before the 2003 World Cup. How could that have happened? How could he be so vain, so stupid, so self-centred to forget about the team? Why did he think he would be bullet proof?

It took me a while to work through my thoughts and emotions, and then to look at what the incident meant to Warney. By that time he was long back in Australia, so I sent him a long email the essence of which was that through his dismissal from the team he had been given a second chance that not all of us are fortunate enough to get in life. If he wanted to take it, he had the opportunity to take responsibility and wear the consequences of his actions. This step, I believed, would be an important step for his future on and off the cricket field.

Keeping the door open and staying in touch, either by phone or e-mail, is crucially important to the coach–star relationship. A star needs to know they can reach you at any time.

In fact, building and maintaining relationships with anyone is hard work, but in the case of sports stars it is a constantly challenging role for a coach, or for those who wish to exert some influence on their life. Wherever and whenever possible, I keep my ego in my back pocket. I don't want to engage in a battle of egos — all that achieves is unhealthy conflict. It immediately severs or at least severely damages the relationship which, in turn, takes a long time to repair. In the meantime, the star does not handle ego denting very well and will generally try to find ways to reinforce their position. In the end no one wins and the ongoing tensions are quite disruptive to the team environment.

To help with this process, it is essential to keep in contact with as many of those people who significantly influence your stars' lives — partners, parents, coaches, friends, peers and managers. I have to admit this could be a 24–7, 365 days a year job!

KEY MESSAGES

1. Try to provide young stars with a balanced life and sport education.

2. Accept that the star is going to bring pluses and minuses to your team.

3. Get to know your stars as best you can — always keep the door open to them.

4. Realise you are only one influence in their lives, so try to get to know them better through others who play a significant part in their lives.

26

Pressure is a myth

PRESSURE IS DEFINED IN the Oxford dictionary as an 'influence or persuasion of an oppressive kind'.

How often do we use this term when we feel 'under the pump' — under pressure? Pressure situations are different for all of us. Some of us really feel under pressure when faced with a computer; some are afraid of heights; for some it might be going to an interview, doing an exam, going on a first date, going for your driver's licence test, or indeed a myriad other situations.

People confront pressure situations differently. For those who struggle in some circumstances, who feel unable to cope and are a bit lost, there are those that deal successfully with the same circumstance because they have previous experience or skills to deal with it. They have developed a plan for coping.

Elite sports people confront so-called high pressure situations continually in a sporting contest. Imagine for a moment being Matthew Hayden and Justin Langer walking out to the middle of the Melbourne Cricket Ground with more than 80,000 spectators cheering and yelling. A big, tall, fast bowler like Steve Harmison is waiting at the top of his mark to steam in and release the cricket ball at close to 150 kilometres per hour, a speed that allows the batsman just quarter of a second to make up his mind about what to do. Both Matthew and Justin know that, apart from speed, they've also got to consider direction and length and one poor decision, one tiny error in the execution of the decision they make, can mean a long return walk to the pavilion.

I think that if any of us were placed in that situation we would all feel under extreme pressure. Remember though that everyone copes with pressure differently, depending on their past experiences. There is a famous quote of Keith Miller's, the former legendary Australian cricketer and fighter pilot in World War II, who when asked about the pressure of playing Test cricket said, 'Pressure, that's not pressure! Pressure is when you have a German Messerschmitt up your arse!'

For Matthew and Justin it is not life and death that they face — although it must seem like it at times. Of course they are nervous and anxious as they prepare for that first ball. But as they've walked to the wicket, they've adjusted themselves to the light and sound, and done their routines, routines that every player has when they arrive at the centre to bring their arousal levels down to a manageable level. It is this process that gives both players best chance of seeing the ball well and making good early decisions.

On the other hand, there are times when it is obvious that situations do get the better of players. Anyone watching Glenn McGrath batting against good quick bowling can clearly see he is uncomfortable, uncertain and lacks confidence in his ability to meet the challenges presented by the bowler. Whereas with the situation reversed, Glenn is totally in control as the bowler with the ball in hand.

So how do these players combat pressure? How do they turn a set of circumstances that would seem overpowering into a challenge where they can test themselves?

There are two major ways that elite performers achieve control over these situations — preparation and experience.

Preparation is about ensuring that all their skills — technical, physical, mental and tactical — have been fine-tuned for all the possible scenarios that they will possibly encounter. They know then that, as they enter the field of competition, they can have confidence in the knowledge that they have done the work. They have a basic plan that allows them to make quality decisions while under the intense microscope of elite sport.

They know that they have tested and re-tested the specialist skills (technical and physical) that their sport demands to be successful. As a result of doing the preparation required for the contest, they know that their mind will not be cluttered with negative thoughts like 'I hope I don't get a good ball first up' or 'don't get out' or 'I hope he doesn't bowl me a certain type of delivery' or 'I don't feel like I have got any rhythm' and so on. Negative thinking serves only to muddle and slow down the decision-making process.

If a player can then add *experience* to his/her *preparation*, the two elements combined feed off each other and permit the player a greater sense of control and an increased likelihood of success. The player knows he/she has been in similar situations before and coped.

For those who cannot immediately add the element of experience to a situation, it is important for them to *trust their preparation,* to back themselves that they have done everything they could have done to give themselves the best chance of succeeding.

The notion of backing yourself is the hallmark of all members of the Australian Cricket Team. All players constantly face new situations, for instance, playing in a new country or on a new ground, playing against a new opponent, or playing a new form of the game like 20/20 cricket. Rather than be pressured or threatened or oppressed by the situation, rather than be confused by negative thinking or that clichéd phrase *fear of failure,* each player takes it on as another means to be able to test their skill, to demonstrate to themselves, their team-mates, the opposition and the world what they can do, knowing that they have done the preparation and have the experience. It's their stage. It's where they perform.

KEY MESSAGES

1. See difficult situations as a challenge rather than a threat.

2. Gain control over those situations by having a plan.

3. Develop your plan by preparation, trusting that preparation, and adding experience when you can.

27

Distractions

DO YOU REMEMBER THOSE times when you were deeply involved in a task? It could have been during an exam, a conversation, driving, reading a book and so on. Then suddenly, a thought, an interruption, a voice or another motorist's horn distracted you from what you were doing and made you realise how involved you had been.

During our 2007 World Cup campaign, we had the opportunity to invite Sir Steve Redgrave to speak to the team. Sir Steve is a five-times Olympic rowing champion (the most decorated British Olympian) and nine-times World champion. He also holds many other records and distinctions in the sport of rowing. Among some very interesting insights he gave us was how he kept *reinventing himself* to remain at the top of his profession. He told us that during a race, which takes about six minutes, he believed he was concentrating on what had to be done for only 50 per cent of the time! He wondered what he could have achieved if he had been able to increase that time to 75 per cent or, in other words, reduce his mind being distracted by a further 25 per cent.

I suspect Sir Steve was a very hard marker of his performances and that his attention to what he had to do during a race was disrupted by little outside interference. Yet an elite sportsperson can ill-afford any such distraction from what he or she is doing. A split second of poor decision-making because the athlete has allowed his or her attention to waver, wander or be distracted can be the difference between winning and losing, success and disaster, and selection or banishment.

Distractions come in all forms. There are those which one might term *environmental*. During the 2003 World Cup, the Australian team was faced with some potentially very disruptive and distracting events prior to the first match. We had temporarily lost two players — Michael Bevan through injury and Darren Lehmann through suspension — and on the day before the game Shane Warne was forced to leave the team because of a positive drugs test to diuretics he had taken in Australia. Here were three of Australia's leading One-Day International players out on the eve of the campaign. Not only did each member of the team feel the loss of these individuals in different ways, but the message that we were vulnerable was also rammed home to us very quickly and constantly by the media, public opinion and those with genuine concerns for the players and the team. Unless we dealt effectively with these distractions, the important first game and possibly subsequent games could be doomed.

In the 1994–95 State season, my first season as coach with Queensland, we were playing our penultimate game against Tasmania in Hobart. An outright win would guarantee Queensland a home final. Three other teams could force us out of the final if any two of them gained outright points and we didn't gain a point in Hobart. At the end of the first day, the Queensland story was gloomy with the Tassie Devils bowling us out for a score in the low 200s and they'd wiped off about sixty of those runs with all wickets in hand by stumps. Watching the players troop from the field that day, one could feel the weight of history being carried into a sullen dressing room. Queensland had not achieved a finals victory since joining the competition in 1926. The ghosts of the past, of which a number of current members had been part, were haunting their every thought. In my opinion at the time, this was a huge *historical distraction* that needed to be exorcised.

In Hobart, the Queensland team, which stood on the precipice of fame, sat quietly and morosely in a cold and lonely dressing room. For all of us there were many emotions and feelings, most of them negative, eating away at everything we had achieved for the season. It was time to exorcise these emotional distractions while the feelings were still raw and before everyone left for the sanctity of their hotel rooms. So I attacked the senior players about how they were behaving; how childishly they were reacting to the day's play; how all season we had been *about the process of playing and not the result.* But all we could think about was what the end result might mean to our chances of playing in a final, let alone hosting one.

I was animated for maybe ten minutes. I was not sure whether I had embarked on the right strategy and certainly not sure what would happen next. Well as it turned out Allan 'AB' Border, who was sitting close to my right, reacted strongly and angrily: how dare I question everyone's commitment! Why shouldn't everyone feel disappointed after a day that promised so much but delivered so little! Of course we are trying, we are trying our guts out! AB went on for ten minutes or so.

At the conclusion of what he had to say I responded with, 'Thank you AB, that is what I was hoping to hear.' That was basically all that was said. We left the rooms. I had a stroll with our long-term physiotherapist, Lindsay Trigar, that night and said that I thought they would be OK, there would be no more distractions. For the next three days, the team played some of their best cricket for the year, guaranteeing a home final and as history now records, beating South Australia to claim the first ever title for Queensland in sixty-nine years.

Apart from the environmental distractions, there are always the personal gremlins, or *individual distractions* that each of us have to deal with daily. As a high-profile athlete, doubts, anxieties and questions are always exacerbated by external forces that seek to expose his/her vulnerabilities. Justin 'Alfie' Langer has always been a player plagued by such forces. Before the 2006–07 Ashes series in Australia, Alfie tormented himself and was tormented externally by comments on whether he should be selected in the team. The feeling was: how much rope should he be given by selectors? It seems he'd had to face similar questions throughout his cricket career. One such occasion was his one hundredth test at Johannesburg, an occasion which should have been an incredible moment of personal celebration and recognition. A player who achieves this milestone is among a very select band of Australian cricketers. Yet as Alfie recalls, his whole being had become consumed by actually reaching this moment. No longer was it about preparing himself for each contest, but the contest was about surviving to become a Test centurion. That became the main motivation of why and how he was playing. He strode onto the field to receive his first ball against a quality bowler, Machaya Ntini, but a bowler whom he had faced numerous times in his illustrious Test career. It is hard to know what happened, and I am sure Alfie still does not remember, but he ducked a short ball which struck him a sickening blow just below the helmet line. He was felled and subsequently counted out for the remainder of the game. He was also medically ruled out for the subsequent tour of Bangladesh because of the seriousness of the blow.

I think Justin now readily admits that he was totally distracted by the thought of reaching one hundred Tests for Australia, joining that very illustrious band of baggy green men. At the same time, I am sure there would have been a certain amount of joy in being able to, jam it up those who had criticised his style of play for so many years — all those who have made his journey so tortuous and testing. But at the crucial moment in that one hundredth Test, his mind was clouded, his ability to be focussed on simply seeing the ball and reacting was impeded.

To some degree the situation was no different for him when facing that first ball of the first 2006–07 Ashes Test in Brisbane. Similar doubts were cast. Was he the same player after his last Test injury? Although he had put together plenty of starts in recent Tests without scoring heavily, were these scores sufficient to justify his position in the team? He had talked of retirement before the series — was he in the right frame of mind?

Distractions

Well, as he had done on most occasions, Alfie proved his detractors wrong. He scored 82 and 100 not out, and was a significant player in setting up a first Test victory. He had put to one side all his distracting thoughts, and channelled his thinking and energies into delivering his skills for the contest at hand. Basically, the solution was simple: he had worked out which thoughts were debilitating and which were liberating.

Steve 'Tugga' Waugh, as I have mentioned in another chapter, was one of the great masters of not allowing any distractions to interfere with the immediate task. Tugga's great skill, and one which I believe belongs to all virtuosos in their chosen professions, was his ability to compartmentalise his life. So when it was time for cricket, in he went. And then once inside the main compartment, he opened the necessary sub-compartment — time to bat, time to be captain, time to bowl or time to relax with his team-mates. There was no room for mind suffocating distractions. In fact Steve would sometimes seemingly entertain distractions. However, these were solely used for the purpose of putting him in a fiercely confronting situation — one where he was under siege, and one where he needed all his skill and resolve to beat off Goliath-type odds. It was from these positions of saving the team, beating the odds and conquering the unlikely that Steve thrived, and played some of his greatest cricket.

Back to the events of 2003 World Cup. The World Cup team took time to absorb what had happened to Warney. Some were sympathetic, some were empathetic, some were angry and some confused — everyone was stunned. But after a few hours of personal and small group thinking through what had happened, and what was about to happen, we gathered to discuss the issue as a team. Clearly, we realised that no matter how much we continued to talk about it — what was right and what was wrong, and how much emotional energy we gave to the situation — it wasn't going to change one thing! Warney was gone and we still had our first game the next morning. All we could do *was control what we could control*, and that was the delivery of our skills against the team we had prepared to play — Pakistan. We resolved that night that as sad an outcome Warney's departure from the World Cup was, it would no longer be a distraction for us. Maybe it would be for other teams who believed we could not win without him...

KEY MESSAGES

1. Consciously identify any distractions and determine which ones are controllable — then deal only with those you can control.

2. Find personal and group strategies to eliminate distractions.

3. If performance is not up to standard, more often than not there are distractions interfering with your approach to preparation and 'game play'.

28

Aura

'CITIUS, ALTIUS, FORTIUS' — FASTER, higher, stronger — words that capture the spirit and aura of the Olympic Games. They encapsulate the magnificent feats of athletes, a history dating back to ancient Greece, and the anticipation and excitement that surround the Olympics every four years. Inside this extraordinary spectacle 'dance' these entertainers of sublime athletic skill.

'Mesmerising', 'spellbinding' or simply making you 'quiver at the knees' — these are some of the responses to the unique aura of supreme athletes. Their mere presence seems to make the whole space around them electric. This aura appears to connect to some raw magnetism.

When I was coaching the Australian Cricket Team there were certain members who possessed this commanding aura, such as Shane Warne, Glenn McGrath, Adam Gilchrist, Matthew Hayden, Andrew Symonds and Ricky Ponting. However, a closer examination of these characters suggests that each individual's aura is almost situation specific. For instance, when Glenn McGrath is standing at the top of his bowling mark, ball in hand, looking ever so confident, and just itching to release a ball of unimaginable difficulty for the opposing batsman, he exudes this aura. Yet if we reversed the situation and put Glenn in his batting gear, making himself ready for what he is about to face, then there is not one flicker of aura that surrounds his frame!

Similarly, Ricky, Adam, Andrew and Matthew bristle with aura on the playing field, but less so away from it. Once out of cricket garb, they command huge respect and admiration from those who meet them and watch them closely, but do they continue to project an aura? I am not so sure.

Shane Warne, on the other hand, possesses some of this magic away from the cricket field. Admittedly, he does have a much larger public presence than most, which is often self-cultivated by statements he makes, or by behaviour that is both socially acceptable and not, as well as the networks with whom he is visibly associated. These provide him some of this mysterious aura off the field.

The Australian Cricket Team has an aura about it. In fact, it is something that the team actively works on and encourages. During the 2003 and 2007 World Cups it was important that we created and nurtured an aura around the team in order to intimidate other teams.

To gain a better understanding about aura and how it is created, a closer look at the Australian team and individuals like Warney will reveal some of the elements.

Firstly, the individual or team must be outstanding performers on their 'stage'. They need to be able to do things others can only dream of, and they need to repeat this time and time again. An aura is not created easily, and it is not a resilient glow initially.

It can easily flicker with poor performances, but once properly in place, it becomes a weapon of immense power to the owner. It glows stronger when an apparent flicker has been overcome under siege or in battle. As has been witnessed on many occasions with the Australian Cricket Team's 'never-say-die' attitude, the team has on numerous occasions fought back from seeming hopelessness to wrestle a miraculous win.

For the mantle of aura to be made stronger and stronger it requires the wearer to be ever vigilant of how and when it can be used. The Australian Cricket Team has found numerous ways in which to add additional filaments to the light. In terms of dealing with the public and sending messages to opposition teams, the media are an important means of projecting the aura.

At the beginning of any Test series, comments made to the media about Shane Warne and Glenn McGrath's previous 5–0 wins, their decisions to target key opposition players, and what new tricks they had in store for unsuspecting batsman, all begin the intimidation of the opposition. Other players would follow with somewhat less bold comments, but nonetheless ones which complemented the two senior maestros.

While words are important, they can only complement actions. And the deeds of the team were not just restricted to what was achieved on the field currently or historically, it was also in clear evidence off the field. The way the team trained; the way it presented itself in public through dress, behaviour and speech; the number of times it was the market leader in its approach to competition — each action strengthens the aura.

In other words, the aura becomes the whole package which makes it real and strong. At an individual level, it is much the same. Shane Warne could not have hoped to have reached his position without his deeds on the cricket field. Opposition players must have nightmares when recalling Warney delivering from the bowler's end; his control over their mind was almost hypnotic, his control of the projectile mercurial and his choice of words or gestures so penetrating.

His burgeoning body shape and his flamboyant, sometimes petulant batting and fielding threatened to damage his aura at times, but Warney is the complete package. He knows exactly how to mend any dimming light. Besides his bowling performances, Shane could wrap the media around his spinning finger whenever he needed. He presented himself in style with dress, manners and vocabulary that allowed him to control or even make the agenda. His eyes would work people over until they were submissive or retreated.

An aura may not be important to all of us, or indeed available to all of us. However, it is another tool in the kitbag.

For a business team, just like a sporting team, competitive advantage in an increasingly competitive market is essential for survival. There are many strategies to achieve this position — aura is simply another one.

KEY MESSAGES

1. An aura is a strategic tool for teams, groups and individuals.

2. It is primarily driven by performance.

3. It can be supplemented by visible actions outside the performance arena, through use of public media and specific, individual personal skills.

29

Expert ... or expertise?

A LONG TIME AGO there was a young student teacher who was given the task of teaching a group of Year 10 students. He thought he was sufficiently smart enough to instruct them in the basics of volleyball. Well, why not? He had played volleyball at university, had done some preparation for the class, and of course he was older and smarter than the students. In his mind and in his approach he was the expert.

Things went along reasonably well even though the students were not really into the class. Then one of the students decided to test the student teacher with a question about the rules of the game — a question that the teacher had not counted on and knew he didn't have the answer. With his supervisor looking on the student teacher didn't want to demonstrate a lack of knowledge, and certainly did not want the class or the supervisor to realise he wasn't the expert which he believed he should be.

So he provided an answer that he knew was not correct, and when pressed by the pupil, he took the dominant position and spoke down to him. This response only encouraged the inquirer, who was then joined by a mocking class, to rebuke the student teacher who was clearly wrong. Now the whole class was offside for the rest of the lesson.

The student teacher was caught in no-man's land — he had taken a stance, a control position and it was too late to admit he was wrong. Neither did he want to demonstrate to the supervisor that he was not the expert and not fully prepared for his subject and his teaching lesson. Fortunately, he was saved by the bell and the class moved on.

That student teacher was me and the incident taught me a valuable lesson. Being an expert is a very difficult role to fulfil. An expert is a very rare breed. And almost by definition, to be an expert one needs to have complete knowledge on the subject and then be able to explain or answer inquiries to the complete satisfaction of the audience.

This experience, and one or two others like it in my formative years of working and teaching, told me that setting myself up as an expert meant that at some point when I least expected it or least wanted it, I was positioning myself for a big fall. So, rather than being regarded as an expert, I tell people that I have expertise in a range of areas. But I am not an expert; I would rather be credible.

I'm constantly asked by critics, the media and by people genuinely interested in understanding how could I coach cricketers of great skill while not having demonstrated a similar skill level myself? They ask questions such as:

'You didn't play very much first-class or any Test cricket, so how did you tell Warne or McGrath how to bowl? What did you tell Gilchrist, Hayden, Ponting or Hussey about batting?'

Well firstly, let me say that I am yet to meet the expert who's played a hundred test matches as a bowler who was both deadly quick and a spinning wizard, batted in all positions, kept wickets throughout and fielded exceptionally in all positions in the middle. Such a person does not exist. But this is the image of the phantom coach held by the critics.

Secondly, I have always felt it to be an advantage not having had to carry a lot of the baggage (good and bad) of a previous life in the Australian Cricket Team. It has allowed me to look at cricket in Australia and around the world from a far more objective position.

And I am sure that coaches in other fields — business, trades, professions and volunteer work — people who have risen from a specific job skill to manage, coach and lead, are not expert in all aspects of their particular field, no matter how broad their experience. So what makes them successful?

There are obviously many factors that bring about success: talented staff, hard work and dedication, vision for the task, timing and opportunity. But one of the key commonalities among successful leaders is that they understand their expertise and limitations.

In my former role as head coach of the Australian Cricket Team, I had a sound knowledge of the technical skills of batting, bowling and fielding; the physical skills needed to play the game;

the mental skills required to succeed as an elite athlete; and the tactical skills required to win games. However, I chose wherever possible to have those who were expert in each area become closely associated with the players. There were the batting coaches, bowling coaches, a fielding coach, a mental skills coach, and personal coaches who certain players would always revert to. And of course, there were the players themselves, who were some of the best coaches of their peers.

To complement these experts, I needed to work out where my skills and expertise should be best utilised. This varied and evolved the longer I spent with the team and was influenced by the fact that I had pretty much the same strong core of players throughout my tenure.

I therefore directed my expertise essentially towards maintaining the success of the team — what needed to be done to allow this Australian Cricket Team to continue to perform at the highest level possible. I focused on:

- Getting the best from people.
- Maximising our amount of resources and their utilisation.
- Knowing the right people to have around the team.
- Being patient (most of the time) in order to influence key decision makers.

I must again stress at this point that my methodology is derived from past experiences which have shaped my philosophy and key principles. It has worked for me in my work situations and over the past thirteen years as a cricket coach for Queensland and Australia. Where it has not worked I have found I have deviated from *who I am* and *the way I do things*.

Finally, don't be an expert, be a servant. When I was coaching Queensland and Australia, I was there to serve the players, the captain, the team and the support staff. In every way, their needs are the highest priority. This means that:

- I put my ego in my back pocket.
- I sacrificed my needs for that of the team, and for individuals.
- I am prepared to be taken advantage of, always believing (naively in a few cases) that the situation will correct itself.

It is without doubt a very frustrating and difficult way of coaching. However, it is how I go about it. My philosophy towards life and the principles that stem from this drive my coaching methods.

KEY MESSAGES

1. Do not be the expert; be credible through the best use of your expertise.

2. Know how your expertise can complement or supplement the expert knowledge in your team.

3. See your role as a coach to serve not to be served.

30

Traditions

Part of the fabric

WHEN WAYNE BENNETT LAUNCHED the twenty-year history of the Brisbane Broncos Rugby League Club he remarked on the enduring values that have been part and parcel of its history from the very first side he coached... twenty years ago.

Embedded within a strong and enduring value system are traditions and symbols, some of which have manifested themselves to be 'values in action'. Twenty years may not seem a long history in which to establish club traditions. However, the weekly team meeting where reviews and awards are made, the early Sunday morning pool recovery ritual, the barbecue at the clubhouse with the fans after a home game, 'Buck the Broncos' stallion proudly galloping the sidelines after hometown tries, the celebration of former players and honour boards listing achievements, the club colours, logos and their appearance at each game — actions like these are all about weaving the tapestry of tradition.

Traditions are a vital link with the past and can provide a springboard to the future. On the other hand, they can act as a heavy weight, holding the team or organisation back from new horizons.

We see many examples of tradition in everyday life — simple things like old family photos and heirlooms; conversations which centre on a theme of 'in my day'; uniforms and ceremonial garb worn by institutions such as the defence forces, universities and the courts; the pomp associated with the doorman of some prestigious hotels; church services and special days of various faiths; the magnificent dresses of brides and their bridesmaids on that momentous wedding day; and national days such as Australia Day, Anzac Day and Remembrance Day — the list goes on ad infinitum.

Why do we cling to some traditions, jettison others, create new ones, and allow some to evolve? Why are they important in our lives, and to our teams and organisations?

Traditions always contain an element of 'that is the way we have always done it' so change is not encouraged. There are patterns, routines, and sets of actions that are always undertaken, and so they give a sense of certainty to people's lives.

Traditions also allow new members of an organisation or team to gain a clear and quick understanding of what it is like to be part of this particular community, to become integrated through abiding by the social mores which have helped to establish the rules, standards and expectations of behaviour and deeds.

Traditions

Traditions are also part of remembering the past — the good, the bad and the ugly. They provide the opportunity to learn from history, and build upon it.

Traditions also allow us to celebrate, provide us some uncommon freedoms from our normal existence, and allow us to fleetingly explore a different world.

The Australian Cricket Team, being part of this monolithic sporting structure that sprawls the world, has some peculiar traditions that educate and imbue players with what it is to be a member of this sporting elite.

There is the team song, reputedly born on an Ashes tour of England and first led by Rod Marsh. It has its roots in Australian lyrics, but has been modified to echo the emotion and spirit of a sporting team revelling in the joy of a successful conquest. It's something distinctly Australian. Most Aussie males revel in sport-related bonding, linking arms together in a raucous dressing room, bursting into a victory song, being Australian. I was fortunate. My first call to voice came after my first Test match as coach. Justin Langer, as he has done for those new to the occasion, scribbled the words on a piece of paper for me and said, 'Mate, you are going to need these.'

The 'baggy green' is also another tradition. The baggy green cap is the ultimate symbol of the Australian cricket team. It is to cricket what the slouch hat is to the fighting spirit of Australian troops. It embodies all the heroes, epic battles, awards and the individual and team records. But more than that, it captures an inner spirit, which sees Australian teams play with aggression, skill, innovation, dominance and a never-say-die attitude. It is what backyard and schoolyard dreams are forged upon. While it doesn't mean that Australian teams are guaranteed to win by simply donning the 'baggy green', it does guarantee that all other opposition teams accord the Australian Cricket Team members huge respect.

Therefore, the awarding of the 'baggy green' cap to a new member of the Australian Test cricket playing family is a sacred act — it can't be given to just anybody and can never be demeaned. To devalue its significance in any way will begin a process of unravelling the fabric of Australian cricket forevermore.

The cap is always presented to a new player by a former player in a small team ceremony at the warm-up huddle on the day of the new player's debut. While every presentation is significant, the older the player who presents the cap, the greater the link to the legion of players who have gone before.

The dressing room stories are another means for traditions to be passed down from player to player and from one generation of players to the next. When I started with Queensland, Allan 'AB' Border had a corner position in the old pavilion dressing rooms. After training, he would ease himself into his corner, beer in hand, and spend an enjoyable hour or so talking to the young members of the team. Some of the stories might have been exaggerated, some even fictional, but all AB's stories were based around what it was like to be an Australian cricketer from when he started in the mid-70s to when he finished in the early 90s.

In my time with the Australian Cricket Team, the dressing-room story-tellers were Justin Langer, Adam Gilchrist and Darren Lehmann. However, the locations for some of these stories are now finding there way into more contemporary settings such as restaurants and coffee shops.

As well as the old traditions, new ones have evolved:

- En-route to the Ashes series in England, the Australian team visits World War I sites at Gallipoli and Villers-Bretonneux.

- Partners and families have become much more involved in the touring life of players. One notable get-together is on the eve of the Boxing Day Test.

- Ricky Ponting has followed the actions of his previous captain and redesigned the blazer worn to toss the coin for a Test match.

- When the Australian Team is in public or at major events it has adopted a 'business image'.

Traditions are an important feature of the Australian Cricket Team. Some, such as the 'baggy green' cap are an integral part of the team. Some are more transient, but are important because they highlight certain values, actions and behaviour. For instance, at the completion of most tours I would make a small presentation to every member of the side. The gift acted as either a thank you from me as coach for the efforts everyone had made before and throughout the campaign; as recognition of the person as an individual, sometimes in a humorous way, but always with a message, and/or was an 'au revoir' until we next met as a group. Some would not be continuing in the team.

KEY MESSAGES

1. Traditions are integral to reinforcing the desired social norms of a team.

2. Traditions are used to provide certainty, remember the past, introduce new members to a team and as a means to celebrate.

3. Traditions are delivered in a range of different ways most appropriate to the team and environment to be created.

31

Generation Y and patience

AS A FATHER OF five who range in age from twenty-four down to thirteen, as a coach of young men who range in age from twenty-one to thirty-five, as a consultant who spends time with employers, and as an observer of my children's friends and acquaintances, I would not like to call myself an expert, but I would like to venture a few thoughts on a few of the characteristics of Generation Y.

My eldest son plays sport at an elite level and is on the edge of achieving an important goal. He is doing everything he believes he can to get there, but for him it is taking too long to jump that final hurdle. There is too much uncertainty and therefore he is putting too many expectations on every performance. The rewards are tantalisingly close. Every day he plays he is reminded of what could be... and the current reality of what is. I am sure he thinks there must be a shortcut through this period — *'If only I can get there now before anyone else, I can secure my position and look to the next rung which is really where I want to be — international honours'.*

One of my daughter's best friends has taken up a job in human resource management having just graduated from university. She is talented and vivacious but comes to the job with no experience. The company, it seems, is throwing her in at the deep end by requiring her to undertake duties that are outside her skills and knowledge base. However, this is often the way in life, business and sport — that things are not what they are supposed to be. If we want to gain knowledge and experience, we have to find ways to deal with what we are presented with. If not, it is time to run away. My daughter's friend is contemplating what her course of action should be, but is tending towards the latter rather than the former. This approach — of not wanting to find out how good (or not so good) you are — is more common among young people than we appreciate.

Within the Australian Cricket Team there have been plenty of conversations with players who are wondering why they have not been given 'a go' when, in their opinion, and in the opinion of others, they are due for an opportunity. One conversation in particular with one of the younger members of the team, Michael Clarke, gave me further cause to ponder Generation Y's lack of patience.

The team was about to embark on the ICC Champions Trophy in India in October 2006. I had arranged to meet Michael for breakfast in our hotel in New Delhi because I was keen to talk about his role during the one-day tournament. However, while the conversation started there, it quickly escalated to Michael's ambitions to regain his Test position. He wanted to be on this tour as he had for the previous one-day tour to Malaysia a month earlier, but his burning desire was to be back in the Test side.

In his view, while he was playing one-day cricket there was little chance that he could impress selectors of his credentials for a Test recall. The only way that he could possibly make an impression was to bat higher up the order for Australia during this ICC event. Coming up was the Ashes series, the series to end all series, and he wanted to be part of the team for the first Test in Brisbane in November. It was all he could think of — he just must be there.

There is certainly nothing wrong with ambition, desire and determination. And there is certainly nothing wrong with a player openly expressing such views. I have always liked Michael's candidness, which some have called precociousness. But he is a young man seemingly always in a hurry. He is effervescent and like the pinball in a pinball machine, bouncing from 'one score' to the next, always lighting up the machine. His energy is boundless!

Some of the employers I've discussed this Generation Y phenomenon with are also experiencing the results. In employing this generation they are finding that they have to:

- Offer larger than normal start-up salaries to gain talented young staff.

- Structure incentives, bonuses and enticing packages to keep a restless young employee.

- Accept questioning by existing longer term and older staff as to why younger, less experienced employees are more important than them.

- Accept young staff members moving on after a short stay because they aren't satisfied with the job or what the company has to offer.

So a quick sift through these anecdotes might suggest some credence to the Generation Y lack of patience theory. But I'm not so convinced.

There is little doubt in my mind that if we want to label someone, some group or some period we can, and we do. We are very good at describing *difference* and being suspicious of this difference.

Take my own experiences of how my parents brought me up. One of their greatest gifts to me, as well as one of their miscalculated mistakes, was to set about making my life easier and better than theirs had been. My parents did not want me to leave school at fourteen years old to find work to supplement a family's income for food, shelter and clothing, as they had to. They made sure I had the best access to education, sport, work opportunities and networks that they could provide.

My wife and I do the same for our children — we try to give them as many opportunities as we can so that their start in life is as good as it can be. But this nurturing style of upbringing may also be part of the problem for this new generation. In many respects life has come easily; it abounds in material extravagances; the nurturing has muddied the waters between right and wrong; responsibility and accountability; it rewards the young and new and seeks to replace old; and it acknowledges experience but champions freshness.

Generation Y and patience

So what can be done to bridge the divide between the generations? Some of the examples I have heard and seen are moving in the right direction. They include:

- Ensuring jobs have different levels, so that employees are always advancing (provided they are meeting the required standards of the job).

- Employers providing more than just remuneration as an incentive — trying to understand the lifestyle needs of their staff and offering ways to assist that makes a difference immediately.

- Recognising that the work team or the sports team will be comprised of a range of people, and that to segregate a group for special attention causes unnecessary conflict.

- Allowing younger people to observe, listen to older people and discuss their backgrounds, ambitions and work practices.

- Providing opportunities for all staff to be involved with community work helping others — whether it be through planting trees, rubbish removal projects or working with charities and not-for-profit organisations helping the disadvantaged.

In the Australian cricket team the formal and informal grouping of the younger and the older players has worked very well for both. For example, Matthew Hayden and Justin Langer have had some sage advice for Michael Clarke, while they have benefited from his ideas, new perspectives and 'bubble'.

Glenn 'Pidge' McGrath has, in part, had his career extended by his willingness to engage with a few of the new young lions like Shane Watson, Mitchell Johnson, Shaun Tait and Ben

203

Hilfenhaus. At the same time, there is no doubt that these players have gained a greater appreciation of the patience, hard work, hard breaks and the wealth of experiences that have made Pidge the legend that he is.

In general, I think there is no doubt that younger people today are more prone to want things to happen for them more quickly than the previous generation. However, this is very much part and parcel of modern everyday living — fast food, fast service, fast cars and fast communications. This generation is simply reacting to what has been provided for them. Great care must be taken then with labels.

It seems our role can be to moderate some of the social excesses, to provide our knowledge and experiences wherever possible, and to keep challenging the thinking of the younger generations in order to bridge the divide.

KEY MESSAGES

1. Be careful labelling all young people as 'Generation Y'.

2. Continue to challenge their thinking in order to keep building their skills.

3. Find ways at work and in less formal settings to have young people and those with more experience associate with each other.

32

Life balance

BALANCE COMES IN ALL shapes, sizes and circumstances: balancing the books, balancing the intake of food with the output of exercise, balancing career and family, balancing self indulgence with care for others and so on.

I think for most of us, we are confronted daily by the 'busyness' of life. Everything seems to be getting quicker, there seems to be more to do and precious little free time to 'smell the roses'.

We certainly found this to be the case as a travelling cricket team. On average the team would spend 220 to 250 nights away from home every year, travelling throughout Australia and the world.

To give you a quick picture of our lives, here's a typical schedule. Starting in April there is a four- to six-week break before individual fitness training starts in late May and continues through to June. Throughout this time the coaching and support staff are completing their planning and budgeting.

From July to mid-August, players move from pure physical activity to skill preparation. At this stage, the players and coaches are doing this work individually or in small groups in their respective states. Of course, some players have been playing over winter, keeping their skills honed in the tedium of English County cricket.

In late August or early September a squad of players and all the support staff will assemble for a small camp, generally in Brisbane. Here, we will do some training and planning for the season ahead — for tours, pre-tour assessments, fit-outs, and administrative, media and promotional requirements.

From early to mid-September the team embarks on overseas tours — generally a one-day series, returning to Australia in late October or early November. This allows some ten to twelve days before the team gathers in Brisbane for the first Test of the Australian summer.

Between November and mid-February the team usually plays five Tests, ten One-Day Internationals and the three-match Chappell–Hadlee one-day series in New Zealand before leaving Australian shores for another overseas series. The series will be of varying lengths and usually consist of both Tests and One-Day Internationals. For players involved in both forms of the game, they will return home by around June or July. Players involved in only one form of the game will travel backwards and forwards to locations based on the timing of their events.

In a normal year the entire team and support staff will have a break for about four weeks before embarking on the next schedule commencing in August or September. It will then follow a similar pattern concluding around the end of April.

Due to the hectic schedule, plus our desire to be not only the best, but also improve our best every day, it was important that we each found our own ways of getting away from the routines of cricket and the constant attention that goes with the territory.

Justin Langer enjoyed writing, as well as meditation. His partner at the top of the order, Matthew Hayden, loved nothing better than surfing or fly-fishing. Ricky Ponting would always find a golf course, Glenn McGrath craved a bit of hunting and Andrew Symonds went bush. Brett Lee and Shane Watson found solace in their music and guitars, Steve Waugh would dive into the local communities while others would group together at various times to take in the local coffee shops (if available). I was happiest when I could run and swim.

It is important to find your place or your space where you can have some free time and do some thinking. It's an opportunity to recharge your batteries, and to look back on what is currently consuming the majority of your time.

There are a few steps that help you to maintain a balance between sport or work and other, equally important, aspects of your life:

Step 1: Understand yourself in terms of where you can go and what you can do to free your mind.

Away from work everyone's lives are so different, circumstances change from year to year and even from week to week. While on tour, modern technology helps a lot through e-mails, phone calls, photos sent home and received from home, the use of Internet phone and so on. All these things are good but, of course, nothing replaces being home.

Step 2: Don't think solely about yourself and that golf round you may be missing out on — put the family first when you have the opportunity.

For me it was all about family. I'd have my time away thanks to the sacrifices my wife and children make. Once home though it was my turn to give back — doing the school drop-offs and pick-ups, taking the kids to sports training, going to the school concert, racing around Brisbane to watch Saturday sport in three or four different venues, helping with homework and just being around.

Step 3: Increase one-on-one conversations and 'be there' in the discussion, not somewhere else.

As I have said, technology is increasingly impacting on our lives. When we're busy we tend to communicate by SMS or e-mails, and we have less 'rich', less 'one-on-one' communications. Why do we find it easier to e-mail than phone and talk to someone? Have we lost the art of conversation? I think it is time to redress the balance.

Ensure that when we are talking with another person, we are listening to what they have to say, and not allow our mind to wander onto other business or be interrupted by the phone. Spend more quality time with people.

Allowing good conversation time with players and support staff is essential to coaching. I found as coach I didn't do enough of it. It was always one area of my coaching that I sought to improve, but one that I could spend all my time on and still fall well short of the mark.

Step 4: Have a positive attitude through doing things that promote the values you cherish.

Do we see the cup as half full rather than half empty? Are we more prone to offering praise than putting others down? There is no doubt that we all can be quick to judge due to our personal beliefs, or information that we have or don't have. I think it's a natural human tendency to define people and things; it provides us with a sense of certainty, even though it may be flawed. Before jumping to hasty conclusions, actively find the means by which more informed opinions and judgements can be made.

Step 5: This final step has been borrowed from Martin Luther King: 'Take the first step in faith. You don't have to see the whole staircase, just take the first step.'

KEY MESSAGES

1. Find your 'free space'.
2. Place family before personal needs when you can.
3. Be *in the moment* with people, avoid distractions.
4. Choose the *half-full* method as the initial assessment.
5. Be proactive for a more balanced perspective.

33

If only men could cry

WHEN MY DAUGHTER LAUREN was advised of her first exam result for her medical degree, she excitedly told me it was a 'seven', the highest grade possible! I said that was great and I was very pleased for her, it was due reward for all the hard work she had put in. Later that day, my wife said to me that Lauren was disappointed at my reaction — that I seemed to get more excited about the achievements of the boys in the family than anything she does.

Of course this was not right, but what I had done was not express the emotions that I felt — I had kept them inside. In part, my response was dictated by the fact that most of the exams Lauren sat for she excelled in, so it was a little bit of 'I knew you would. I knew you would handle whatever was put in front of you as you have always done.' Instead of acknowledging and displaying my feelings of pride, I chose a more dispassionate, disinterested approach which reflected my knowledge of her as my daughter of twenty-one years, rather than just looking at that particular moment in time.

How often do we do this — suppress our emotions because showing them is not the done thing? Men and boys are both incredibly good, or bad, depending which way you look at it, at holding inside their emotions, because the male gender has been socially constructed to be tough with no weak edges.

On my first Ashes tour of England in 2001, we had played exceptionally well throughout the series. We had won the first three Tests, lost the fourth, and were about to head into the fifth and final Test at Lords. There was one last County game to be played before the Test, and Steve Waugh was fighting against time to be fit, Michael Slater was dropped because of his erratic performances, and so there was an opening batting spot available.

Justin 'Alfie' Langer had been the unlucky player at the beginning of the tour when Matthew Hayden and Michael Slater had been given the task of opening the batting. Alfie had to endure watching his team-mates retain the Ashes while he was given limited opportunities to convince everyone that he should be in the team.

But at this last County game Justin had this chance to score some runs, enough to warrant inclusion alongside Matthew Hayden. We bowled Sussex out on day one and Alfie only had to survive until stumps with the prospect of batting as long as he wanted next day. Sadly, he lasted only a few balls — out for a duck.

I sat near him in the bus that evening on the drive back to the hotel, a more dejected and lost soul I have never seen. As we got out of the bus, Adam Gilchrist and I grabbed Alfie and convinced him to come and have a drink at the bar. After a couple of beers and Alfie beginning to get back to his normal self, Adam left for the safety of his room, some room service and a good night's sleep to be ready for the next day.

Alfie, however, was now not batting the next day, and I needed to talk with him, so the beers kept coming.

As we talked, with a little help from the alcohol, Alfie's emotions began to show through. He felt betrayed by Steve Waugh and me because we had not backed him in the selection room, as he had always backed us with his trust and loyalty. As the tour wore on and he seemed to play himself further and further out of contention for recall, he felt he had lost the chance to ever represent Australia again. He would never again be able to don the 'baggy green'. In his mind he had lost his reason for being, as cricket was his world. It was what he had wanted since he was a young child and now it was gone, unfairly snatched from him. He said to me, 'I feel as though my heart has been ripped out.'

Fortunately the bar closed, which forced us to stagger up the staircase to his room. As Alfie opened the door I gave him a big hug. Firstly because he needed one and secondly because he had the courage to get his feelings out and not continue to do what he had done all tour — perpetuate the image of being the 'tough' male.

I asked him if he was given a chance to play in the final Test, could he do it? He replied, 'Just give me the chance!' Now it may have been a slurred response, but it came from a heart that was beating again with passion and pride and a boyhood dream of opening the batting for Australia. He was ready to play, irrespective of the fact that he hardly scored a run all tour.

History shows we won that final Test. Steve Waugh miraculously played and made 150 to boot; Alfie made a century and Australia steamrolled England by an innings. What history doesn't record was the smile that never left Alfie's face, right from the moment his name was read out for inclusion in the team until the end of the match.

Interestingly, after Alfie had disclosed his feelings, I met with the other players who had fulfilled bench roles for most of the tour — Damien Fleming, Colin Miller and Wade Seccombe. While not expressing the same depth of emotion and despair, all to a man were carrying the heartache of not being selected, but had not wanted to share their feelings with anyone as they might be viewed as being soft. It was also a fact that many players who were more secure in their position in the team were completely unaware that you could actually feel like that. Why would you not be happy being on one of the best tours, a coach tour through the UK for the Ashes.

Michael Slater, whose position became vacant after the fourth Test, suffered from similar emotional isolation, although his circumstances were complicated by what was later diagnosed as a mental illness. Steve Waugh, myself, and a number of team members all tried to provide what help we could as Michael began to suffer bouts of anxiety. However, the tough male facade did not allow us to penetrate. I know that by the later stages of the tour when Michael's behaviour was very erratic, Steve Waugh, the team manager Steve Bernard and myself were trying to work out how to organise professional help for him — if not in England at least for when he arrived home.

While Michael's case was at the extreme end of emotional dysfunction, complicated by illness, touring life confronts all of us emotionally at different times and in different ways.

Obviously, there are things that all of us like to keep private and not share with even our closest loved ones. I think how Glenn McGrath has managed somehow to maintain his favourite expression of 'Never better!' when people inquire as to his health, his wife Jane's wellbeing, his career and future selection. I cannot imagine the myriad emotions he must have carried within, and how they impacted on him as he returned to a lonely hotel room in Nagpur, Gwalior, Chittagong or Bulawayo, or even to the seemingly safe surrounds of Quay West in Melbourne.

But as with all big families, good teams, and large groups that live together for long periods, there are a couple of players within the Australian team who are better at displaying and expressing their emotions than others. To some degree these guys who have moments of outpouring openness and honesty, release a valve for everyone.

Adam Gilchrist sheds tears of joy and sadness, and has done so as long as I have known him. He is one man who shares a lot of his soul with the team or individuals at certain moments, and this has made him almost the custodian of the 'emotional glue' that helps bind a team together.

Shane Watson, too, is prone to a burst of tears and releasing some heartfelt emotion. From the team's perspective, it's good to see in one of the new generation the propensity to be open with feelings in a male environment.

In the end it is not about who cries or who doesn't, or who can talk more about what they feel inside and who can't. It is about men and boys being more in touch with their emotions and having the courage to be able to express them. It is also about other males, peers and friends accepting and understanding this method of expression. In many cases the male form of expression takes on the guise of aggression — aggressive language, aggressive behaviours and physicality. Such expression is a definite sign of emotional and personal immaturity — not having a way, a strategy or a skill to deal with a set of circumstances and hiding those inabilities behind a shield of hostility.

It would seem that finding mechanisms to handle internal and external emotional conflicts is an essential part of becoming a more rounded athlete, as well as person. Using mentors, being open with peers, use of professional counsellors and of course, closest loved ones, will all be of great assistance along this path.

If only more men could express their emotions better then I am sure the world would be a different place.

KEY MESSAGES

1. Recognise all of us have emotional abilities and disabilities, especially males.

2. Facilitate a work or living environment that allows and respects emotions to be part of the communication landscape.

3. Constantly develop, initiate and support mechanisms of emotional expression and exchange within this environment.

34

Silver linings

THE YEAR 1998 WAS a disastrous season for English County Cricket club Middlesex. Here was a proud club with a great history, a lineage of English stalwarts and its home on the hallowed turf of Lords — yet it found itself at the bottom of most competition tables.

This had been the season of expectation. The team had some good young players, some very experienced players, some Test players and a coach who was going to transform their past mediocre performances into some silverware come the end of the season — just as he had done in his first year with the Queensland Bulls.

For me, it was an exciting experience and I embarked on the task with great gusto. I attended a training camp in Portugal (which had already been arranged by the club), where I interviewed all the players who attended, as well as the coaching staff. We collaboratively addressed some of the obvious cultural changes that were needed to move forward and reviewed personal and team targets for the season. Overall, the ten days spent offshore seemed to be successful and the blueprint from this was presented to the three England team members, Angus Fraser, Mark Ramprakash and Phil Tufnell, when they returned from their tour of the West Indies.

The presentation went without a hitch until the conclusion of the meeting when everyone had adjourned for an 'I'll-drink-to-that pint of bitter'. The club coach Ian Gould approached me and said that the county captain, Mark Ramprakash, would like to speak to me.

As I was new to this English County scene there were things that I did not understand. Firstly, Mark had just been anointed captain after taking over from the larger-than-life, if not legendary, Mike Gatting, who had basically run the Middlesex Club his way for the last fifteen years or so. Secondly, Mark was intent on holding down his England spot, so he needed to know that he was in control of his destiny. Thirdly, even though we had agreed to abandon the special privileges provided to Test players so there would be a degree of equality within the team, the class system was still well and truly alive.

Mark's first words to me were, 'You don't change the rules of the club. The players don't change the rules of the club. If there are to be changes, I am the only one to make them!' With that he left and the work we had done over the past couple of days seemed to have been torpedoed. Still, I was one not to be denied as I felt the changes were necessary for the club to move forward, and this thinking was shared by a majority of players and staff, particularly the younger players. So, rather than abandoning the idea, I felt that I could gradually bring Mark around to understanding the benefits to the players, the team, and the club.

Alas, time proved I was not going to change Mark's view of the world, and so tensions between him and myself became obvious to everyone. Middlesex's early season promise dissipated within a couple of weeks and the club hurtled to ignominious positions in all competitions. The club and I reached the only conclusion that could be reached — that while Mark remained captain, there was no place for me. So my contract would be terminated at the end of the season. My family, who had visited during school holidays, had returned home, and the last nine weeks of the 1998 season were some of the loneliest and longest days of my coaching life.

While in the midst of this maelstrom of bitterness, frustration, anger and confusion, I could only see the negatives. *Why had I bothered? What a terrible system English County cricket was! How can smart people not see that the culture needs changing?*

But as the initial hurt disappeared, as the battered ego began to repair, and as I continued to have conversations with many good people in and around the club, players included, I realised that if I was prepared to look for them there were plenty of lessons to be learned about myself and about my approach to coaching.

Here were the 'silver linings' of my experiences:

- I had tried to change the culture of a club and a system too quickly.
- I had not spent initial time with 'key' players such as Ramprakash, Gatting, Brown, and a couple of behind-the

scenes administrators, to be very clear on my role and how I would approach that role.

- Develop a strong and binding relationship. Hence I could not 'sell' the benefits of what I was trying to do.

- I had not fully committed myself to the cause of Middlesex, as I was doing the job while still employed at Queensland Cricket as head coach of the Bulls.

I had a similar experience as coach after Australia lost the 2005 Ashes in England. We had travelled to England with high expectations of sweeping England and Bangladesh aside in the one-day series, and then crushing an upbeat England side in the Test series.

While we staggered a little through the initial phases of the tour due to injury, off-field misdemeanours and some inconsistent on-field performances, we still managed to tie the one-day series with England, win the best-of-three one-day series against England, and then travel to Lords to win the first Test. From then on it was hold onto your seats for an amazing ride of Test cricket. Runs, wickets, drama, controversy — it had it all. Those at the ground and the television and radio audiences were treated to some of the most amazing scenes such as Lee and Kasprowicz almost snatching victory in the second Test at Edgbaston after McGrath had trodden on a ball on the first morning of the game and was ruled out of that and the next Test with an ankle injury.

Then, in the second innings of the third Test, Giles and Hoggard did what the England top order was unable to do by chasing a small total and scoring runs to win the contest.

England played all over Australia in the fourth Test, but Ricky
Ponting played the innings of his career, as did Lee and McGrath,
to deny England victory and a series win.

And finally, the fifth Test at The Oval. England needed only
a draw to regain the Ashes which they duly achieved. But not
before Australia had made a charge and the weather intervened
to alter the balance of the game — and this was topped off by
Warney's problematical dropped catch from a hesitant Pietersen
early in his innings.

The inevitable daggers that are always raised over successful
players, teams and coaches were plunged deep. Our critics
finally had the means to unleash their vitriol — an unforgivable,
unthinkable Ashes loss. Even Cricket Australia could not repel
those that wanted answers. A review was called for.

Coach, captain and players were all subjected to the
machinations of the review committee. The silver lining lay in
the opportunity of being forced to think through the coaching
process, the commitment to the job and the relationships that
would enable me to continue in the job. If I had not explored
these thoroughly or, indeed, found I was inadequate in any one of
them, I would not have been able to continue my role.

A silver lining does not always have to be found in a personal
dark cloud. In 2007, I was fortunate to be involved with Mal
Meninga and the Queensland State of Origin team for the final
game in Brisbane. The match was billed as the first State of Origin
whitewash of the New South Wales 'Blues' since Fatty Vautin's
Queensland 'Maroons' in 1995.

Mal had invited me to talk at the team dinner on the eve of the third game. In speaking with Mal, almost all of the players were already in new territory — leading 2–0 in a series and going into a game as favourites. Add to this the expectation of the game being a 'whitewash', I felt it was more than likely that these young guys would be lulled into placing result over process. The situation was placing huge expectations and distractions on a team that had avoided most of that baggage until now. It was likely to result in a lack of respect for the strength of the opposition.

My fears were founded as, although the Maroons fought and defended valiantly, the result went the way of the Blues. However, Queensland still won the series 2–1. The silver lining for the team was that all those players and staff had now experienced being the 'favourites', being in uncharted waters, being odds-on to make a clean sweep and being decimated by injury… and yet still came so close to winning.

No matter what happens to us in life, in sport, in business, whether it's good or bad, there are always long-term lessons to be learned. They're the silver linings… if we're prepared to look for them.

KEY MESSAGES

1. There is always a lesson to be taken from any situation.

2. Take time to look at what has happened and search until you find the silver lining. There is always one.

35

So you want to be a coach?

I HAVE BEEN ASKED time and time again: 'What have you done as a coach that other coaches have not? What makes your style different to other coaches? What has enabled you to take a successful team and make it better?'

These are difficult questions to answer, as I, like most other coaches, do not spend time trying to compare my coaching style to others, especially those who have preceded you. The players, support staff and the administration are the people best placed to make valid comparisons.

Nonetheless, I will try to pinpoint some of the things I believe have been important to my success as a coach.

Firstly, let me eliminate some of the givens which definitely impact upon one's coaching, but over which there can be little control. Some of these factors are:

- Talented and gifted athletes — I have certainly been fortunate to have been associated with an Australian cricket team that has had some unbelievable players in its ranks.

- Timing and opportunity — life is often about being in the right place at the right time (or vice versa) and then making the most of the opportunities that present themselves. Taking over the Queensland Cricket Team after Jeff Thomson in 1994, and then the Australian Team after Geoff Marsh in 1999, were wonderful times to be associated with both.

- Early runs on the board — gaining immediate success is a powerful medicine for keeping the lurking critics away, and provides time to settle into the role. It also adds credibility to those whose decision it was to install you as coach in the first place, making them stronger allies.

- External environment — in addition to the critics who are prowling, waiting to pounce on any sign of weakness, there are the many opposition teams. How advanced they are in their planning and team development will determine their capacity to respond to changes presented by another team and its new coaching regime.

- Resources — coaches will benefit from additional spending on players, staff, equipment, programming, research and medical support provided to the team.

However, if these were the only factors that contributed to the success, then I would have to agree with some of those critics who ask 'Why do we need a coach? Coaches are just for getting you from point A to point B.' Obviously, there is more to it than that.

Let me outline some of the factors which, for me, are the highest priorities, and hopefully these may provide an insight into some points of difference.

Self

Some of my earliest feedback from those who managed and coached me was that I was not assertive enough, did not have enough 'mongrel' in me. I took this on board as a young manager of staff and tried to work out how to be stronger in my decision making, in my conversations, and in my presentation. I lacked a certain confidence in myself due to my upbringing and personality — I wouldn't claim success and I found it difficult to accept compliments and accolades. At the same time, if something wasn't working as it should, I would first look at my performance and think I was the major contributor to the situation. Like most people, I needed to be liked, and one way to do this is to be the fall guy. As I matured through the fatherhood of five children, different work placements, education and a range of people and projects, I gained a better appreciation of who I really was.

The Queensland Bulls coaching job was the catalyst for me becoming much clearer about who I was, my philosophies and my principles, and therefore how I operated best. Being assertive is still not one of my preferred styles — it's not me — although now I can be if the need arises. I am better at recognising which situations demand assertiveness and which don't. On top of this, I better understand how to deliver assertiveness. I back my judgement in most circumstances now — provided that I remember I'm generally far better off not reacting immediately, and letting things wash over me so that intuition is mixed with a healthy blend of thinking time.

I am very much a *processes* coach as opposed to a *results* coach; that is, I am never driven by results. I clearly understand that most people, who assess my performance and that of the team, are mostly looking at the bottom line, hence results need to be achieved. However, for me to gain those results, I am totally driven by the process of getting there. I firmly believe that teams which strive only for the bottom line may achieve success, but it will be short-lived. There will be no structures on which to lay the foundations for success over the long-term.

Standards

When I first became coach of the Queensland Bulls and then Australia, my opinion of both teams was that they had only scratched the surface of what their capabilities could produce. It was with this belief that I approached each task — raising the standards of everything about the team. As an approach it was not temporary; it was maintained throughout my tenure. I was always looking for ways to improve everything we were doing on and off the field.

In order to do this, I would live in the future as well as the present. I'm sure my approach was frustrating for many people at various times as it seemed I was more concerned with the so called 'big picture' than dealing with what was at hand. In fact there was many a time when the administration told me quite bluntly that I was simply the coach of the national team, nothing more, nothing less. Yet if I was to coach the Australian team, the only way to ensure that standards kept improving was to look ahead and understand what was required. Working back from that future goal provided me with the strategies to move the team from the present along the path of continual improvement.

Relationships

First and foremost, my task as a coach is to help people wherever possible to be better people, which I believe then impacts directly on their cricket. When talking with other organisations about high performance teams and high performance coaching, I ask two key questions:

- How much do they value people?
- How well do they know their people?

Valuing people can be demonstrated in so many ways, such as:

- Listening to them.
- Giving them first priority on your time.
- Being an advocate for their needs.
- Individualising their specific training.
- Providing them with some slack when it is appropriate.
- Providing them with admonishment when appropriate.
- Knowing their family.
- Always being there for them in good and bad.
- Influencing other people to see their strengths.

This is a chicken and egg statement, but it's the key: *In order to properly value people you must know them very well. But to know them very well (as a coach) you must value them.*

It takes a lot of time to establish strong relationships with each person with whom you interact. In fact, I've always felt that no matter how much time I gave to the players and staff, I never spent enough time with them.

Vision

To deal with the present and know what strategies to employ going forward, I also needed to live in the future. It is always much easier to only deal with the present and respond to whatever is then thrown up at you. Certainly from a playing perspective, this is in part very true and very important. There's an old acronym of 'KISS' which stands for 'keep it simple, stupid', and players, staff and administrators would regularly send me this message.

In the micro-detail of playing the game — that is, dealing with the decision that needs to be made on each ball whether you're a batter, bowler, fielder or captain — you need:

- A clear head devoid of any complicating thoughts.

- Confidence in your ability to make the right decision due to training and experience.

- To back yourself 100 per cent and respond intuitively and automatically to the complexity of the situation.

Once a ball has been played, you need to repeat this approach ball after ball after ball. As soon as players or the team do not play in the moment they get ahead of themselves and become vulnerable. In other words, when their clear head becomes filled with distractions, there is every chance they will make the wrong decision or execute the right decision poorly. This in turn erodes personal confidence and the ability to back themselves 100 per cent. For the coach then, it is a balancing act between dealing with the present but keeping an eye to the future.

Team

Even in a side as strong and as harmonious as the Australian Cricket Team, I always felt I had to keep working at reminding people about what the word 'team' meant. In the fantasyland of international elite sport there are plenty of super egos and an abundance of selfishness mixed in with a lot of insecurities. Everyone works very hard to get to this elite level, and once there the trappings that accompany this highly charged, highly visible and highly paid world are irresistible. It's only human that individuals do whatever they can to protect their time at the top, and if their grip on the top spot is loosened by poor performances, age or injury, then human nature tells them that they had better start looking after number one.

Some players and staff come from a previous culture that might have paid lip service to what the word 'team' means and what 'team-mates' do for one another. While I admit to some bias, it did appear that some of the Queensland players, Andy Bichel, Mike Kasprowicz and Andrew Symonds have a clearer understanding of the term in all its nuances. They are just as passionate and determined as the next player to be part of the Australian team, even if they are not in the running for selection. But as Andy Bichel says when the twelve-man team is selected, he would rather be twelfth man than thirteenth.

Even though Andy holds the record for being twelfth man for Australia (nineteen times) he always goes about his preparation as if he was playing. He is determined to show his peers, his captain and his coach 'that if you don't pick me for this game I'm ready for the next'. In doing so he gives his team-mates the opportunity for the best possible preparation. He waits until everyone has completed their training sessions before he asks for any additional work. During the sessions he is a bundle of energy, ensuring no one senses his absolute devastation at being left on the bench again. He is totally concerned for the welfare of all his team-mates (although secretly hoping that one of his bowling mates will go down injured).

Throughout the game he makes it his business to wait on all the players hand and foot, anticipate their every need and not display any sign of disappointment for fear it may hover as an infectious pall of bad karma over the team. He is there to celebrate with those that return good performances, and also there to support those who have missed out. Very importantly, his care is totally genuine; there is nothing superficial. However, he also organises himself and those around him, to help him maintain his level of skills. He has been around enough teams to know that opportunity always comes knocking, but the player needs to be ready to take it!

Culture

Trying to keep the right culture is the hardest job, and the most time consuming because it is in everything we do or say or act or don't do or don't say or don't act. If it was only me that was responsible for the management and delivery of culture, there would be a modicum of control. But the team culture is delivered by everyone, in particular the leaders.

The Australian Cricket Team was fortunate that through the presence, actions and behaviour of its leaders an appropriate team culture was reinforced daily. As a coach though, it's essential to keep the radar scanning day and night for signs of decay. If detected, then it's important to take steps to eradicate it. For example, a player who stays out late drinking is offensive to a team culture. In the position these young players find themselves — high profile, wealthy, good looking — they are spotted nearly everywhere they go. So to stay out late drinking, while not a social crime, attracts unnecessary and unwanted attention. This spotlight on elite athletes linking them to poor social attitudes, irresponsible behaviour and setting poor examples for all young people to follow, is like a knife that stabs right through the heart of team culture.

The strength of the team culture to resist these moments of poor choice are shown by the ability of others in the group to assume control of the situation and prevent controversy.

Family

Family has always been most important to me. Family will always take precedence over cricket, work or social time. Family displays all the values and traits that a coach wants impregnated into his team. I am very much a 'softie' when it comes to a player or staff member coming to me and asking for a bit of extra leeway due to something very important on the home front.

Control

I have always tried to allow the issue of control to rest with the team. I want them to learn from everything they do, rather than taking the easy way out and pointing the finger in the direction of the coach or others who have made decisions on behalf of the team. This has left me open to criticism on many occasions for not being in control, for allowing undisciplined behaviour and for not providing leadership when it is most needed. However, knowing the players and the team I was always confident that they would self-correct given time and the appropriate guidance. Unfortunately, Australian cricket has too many figureheads: the coach, the captain, the chairman of selectors, the manager, the General Manager (Operations), the Chief Executive Officer and the Board, all of whom believe at some point or in certain situations they are in control. This continues to provide confusion for all those subjected to the inadequacies of this system.

People

For all these thoughts and words, for all the theories that exist on leadership, management, coaching and parenting, coaching is all about what exists between the lines. It is not about what is said, but about:

- What is not said.
- When something was said and why.
- How it was said — with pauses, high voice, low voice, use of analogy or directly personal.
- Where it was said — in isolation, over coffee or in passing.

So you want to be a coach?

Coaching is not a 'how to' manual; it is not about following a set of rules or directions; it's all about people. And people demand to be treated with great respect. Each is an individual, each has their own world and tries to have that in harmony with everything and everybody else around them. They are constantly subject to the uncertainties and vagaries of life which affect their decisions, emotions and needs. The role of the coach is to listen to this diversity and interpret all the signals in order to produce the best possible outcome for the person being coached.

What a challenge! But what an unbelievably exciting and satisfying occupation!

Bob Woolmer was a pioneer coach in many ways. He took on incredible challenges, first with South Africa, then in his role of coaching coordinator for the ICC associate countries development program, and finally with Pakistan. He constantly challenged himself with his coaching techniques, his adoption of technology, his mammoth personal literary investigation into how to improve playing the game, and understanding cultures around the world. I have nothing but admiration for him and only wished I had taken the opportunity to express my sentiments far more precisely in the conversations we had as coaches of opposing teams.

36

Underneath the Southern Cross I stand

AS I SIT GAZING out at one of the great spectacles of the world, the Sydney Harbour, decorated impressively by the Harbour Bridge, the Opera House and a striking blue expanse of water, I cannot but help think (a little ethnocentrically) what a fabulous country I live in.

And high on the list of Australian wonders is its sporting legends. Over the past 90 Tests, I have had the great privilege, the honour, the once-in-a-lifetime experience of being associated with so many special players. The Waugh twins, Darren Lehmann, fast bowlers like Damien Fleming, Andy Bichel and Mike Kasprowicz, and others like Simon Katich, Colin Miller and Greg Blewett — the list goes on.

However, in my final few months of coaching the Australian team, I was able to witness the retirements of two of the greats of world cricket, Shane Keith Warne (cap number 350) and Glenn McGrath (cap number 358). With the passing of time I believe these two players will grow larger and larger in Australian folklore. However, standing tall beside them (and I am certain he will be pleased to read this line) is, in my opinion, another legend, Justin Langer (cap 354), although the game will not necessarily record his deeds this way.

When asked to list the greatest highlights he could remember as a player or a captain Ricky Ponting summed it up for me when he said Warney and Pigeon. He said there were too many moments to remember and that he couldn't put one higher than another, but what he could say was that they were always the go-to men when something special was required. When a match needed to be won, or we needed an event to swing the momentum our way — both these men were always there and rarely, if ever, let the captain, team or country down.

There have been many superlatives and stories written about Warney, also know as the Spin King or the Sheik of Tweak, but three things about his career stand out for me. Firstly, he has changed one of the classic elements of the game, the leg-spin. Secondly, he has an incredible ability to 'compartmentalise' his cricket and focus on the moment. And thirdly, he has shown incredible durability.

I believe greats in any walk of life are defined by their ability to do and achieve things that no one else has been able to do. They do this with skill — technical, physical, mental and tactical. For budding leg-spinners to graduate through the ranks of junior cricket, to club, then to representative honours, the Warne brand of leg-spin is the benchmark.

Warney has certainly placed spin bowling on the world stage. Along with Muttiah Muralitharan, he has set a standard, an expectation of what a leg-spinner should be which is outside the grasp of all those who try. Terry Jenner, Shane's coach and mentor, described it best when he said, 'It is not about where the ball lands, it's all about *how* it arrives there.'

However, to do all this Shane has to be ready to play day in and day out. I asked him one day what his secret was, and as usual for Warney it was just a commonsense approach. He endeavours to arrive at every game day happy and fresh. He deals with his life the day and night before. He clears everything off his plate no matter how long it takes, so that when he arrives at the cricket ground he is able to lock off all the other compartments in his life and just live in the cricket compartment.

This ability to compartmentalise one's life is one of the key attributes to any great performer. It requires incredible mental control to be able to absorb oneself totally in the contest or performance for the time one is there, while being impervious to the rest of the world.

Durability is a trait that has made Shane what he is. Physically, he has suffered a number of injuries. Emotionally, he has been put through the wringer many times. He has played under four captains without being given the chance to lead his country. He has had three Australian coaches who have all had different approaches. Yet throughout his long service, he has constantly sought ways to improve his unique skills. Young cricketers receive masses of advice as their playing career develops and to survive they need to develop a filter that enables to take on the advice that benefits them and reject the advice that is confusing or takes them nowhere.

In the coaching context Warney and I are different people — different backgrounds, different likes and dislikes — we occupy different worlds. What we share is a love of cricket, an enormous pride about representing our country, a never satisfied approach to personal performance, and an unquenchable thirst for the Australian Cricket Team to be the best in the world.

While these may be the general visions and goals we share, there is no doubt we approach them very differently. Often this has been interpreted as an ongoing battle of wills between coach and player. But for the majority of time I viewed our differences as a healthy part of the development of the team. It is vital to have different personalities in a team — management of these different personalities is the key. Inevitably, there will be conflict between personalities, but the trick is to turn it into healthy conflict which works to the benefit of all, as opposed to unresolved conflict which spreads like a cancer throughout the team.

Which brings me to Glenn 'Pidge' McGrath, the other great recent retiree. Here is a man of such experience, such knowledge and revered by all his team-mates. I cannot recall a situation where I have seen or heard Glenn in direct conflict or confrontation with someone in the Australian cricket family. He prefers to remain silent, attempt to interpret or arbitrate in order to gain a resolution. If all that doesn't work, he then just puts it down to the minds or deeds of 'young fellas'.

If Warney is the genius of spin bowling, then Glenn is the template of fast bowling. He is the mechanical model for all to emulate. Again like all greats, he keeps the game very simple. He has checked, re-checked, double checked and triple checked his game on the international stage many times over. And it is the same result — same rhythm in his run-up, gather, arms high, pull down and get through the crease. From here it is top of off stump, remain patient and force the batsmen into error. He is an understated colossus.

Pidge is almost a coach's dream athlete. He knows his game exceptionally well. He knows how to prepare himself. He knows when his action or his body does not quite feel right. He knows instinctively in a match what is required of him and how he will use his skills to deliver the game plan. He has an incredible memory for detail which serves him very well during the pressure cooker atmosphere of Test and One-Day International cricket. He doesn't complain whether bowling into the wind, bowling when totally fatigued, bowling with injury or bowling on a featherbed pitch with an old ball. Pidge will find a way because that's what he does — he leads the Australian attack. He prefers to operate in 'old school' mode to some degree, which means cricket is about playing and that is where your individual game is refined and developed. Training has its place, but the game is the real deal.

But Glenn, like Warney, could not have survived for so long without continually seeking to improve himself. It may not be noticeable in any statistics, but he had spent a lot of time over the past three to four years on his batting and spent time with our specialist fielding coach, Mike Young, on his fielding. He spent additional time on his fitness to allow him to be the resilient, reliable, run-in all day bowler that was one of his trademarks.

I said *almost* the coach's dream — well, there are times that his mischief does test the patience of the coaching staff. Whether at a team meeting, a team drill or a function, his love of the lighter side of life gets the better of him and we all pay for it.

There are insufficient superlatives in the dictionary for Glenn McGrath, but that's never been of concern for him. It has always been about playing the game he loves, playing at the highest level of competition, and enjoying the friendship and camaraderie of all those that he has played with and against. He always has the same response to the general question of how are you going mate? It always comes back, 'Never better!' I am certain that will be the term used to describe Glenn when other bowlers from the past or the future are compared with him.

They say good things come in small packages and it is not all about quantity, rather it is all about quality. Well for me Justin 'Alfie' Langer is quality through and through — it courses voluminously through his veins. He is a man of character, a flannelled warrior, the first man picked to have beside you in the trenches. He leads our team song, not because he is one of the few people who can stand on the table and not bump his head on the many low dressing room ceilings, but because he doesn't set a ceiling to his game.

Alfie is a perfectionist. Even during his last Test he was still talking about his technique and working on his catching and throwing. He has been one player who has been seemingly under the constant threat of being dropped over his entire career. Yet he has withstood the continual criticisms. He has achieved what few players can boast, over 100 Tests for Australia, twenty-three Test centuries and formed one of the most successful opening batting combinations in history of cricket with his great friend, Matthew Hayden.

His favourite word is respect: respect of the game and its traditions, respect for your team-mates, especially those that have served their country with distinction over a time, and finally respect for yourself. Alfie believes that you should never let yourself down nor let your standards slip. I first coached Alfie at Middlesex when he began his stint at the club's hallowed home ground of Lords. At one of our first training sessions it snowed. Two players remained on the park with the coach — Justin Langer and Gus Fraser. Alfie wanted some batting practice so Gus obliged. All their team-mates were crowded into the warmth of the dressing room.

Justin Langer will always have a special place in my heart as a person who has always got up one more time than he was knocked down.

The memories of these three great athletes will always be with me.

37

Beyond boundaries

THERE IS A MIX of principles which connect through everything I do, and while that encompasses such things as vision, planning, organisational culture, stretching beyond boundaries and so on, essentially, at the core of it all, is consideration of the individual. It is from this point that managing, coaching, leading other people can begin.

Add to that the need to develop appropriate physical fitness regimes for individuals and teams; the need to have effective planning and strategy approaches to gain competitive advantage; the very difficult task of improving the decision-making capacity and ability of players; and ensuring that players and support staff with different backgrounds and personalities exist harmoniously within a team environment, and one begins to get an appreciation of the coach's role and why systems and processes, for me, are crucial.

1. Developing the person

When coaching a team, I have always been concerned for the

team members as individuals first and a player or fellow support staff member second. I firmly believe by trying to get to know the whole person individually I can be of far more help than simply putting them into a defined space called 'player' or 'physio' or 'trainer'. There's no doubt that this approach takes more time and energy, and it's always made me feel that I was not putting enough time into the job.

By adopting this approach there are also plenty of frustrations, due to the fact that the coach is only one influence in the life of each individual. Partners, parents, managers, close friends, other coaches and other significant influences all occupy a percentage of the individual's mind, providing direction, counsel, support, love and baggage.

Depending how strong the relationship is between the coach and individual, the amount of influence short- to long-term will vary. Ultimately it is the individual who chooses how much they want to give of themselves in the relationship.

From a coach's perspective, there always needs to be a gap or buffer zone between him or herself and the person being coached, as there will be times when the coach needs to be the school principal, times when the coach needs to be the most trusted, loyal and supportive person in the world (a surrogate parent), and all the situations in between.

So the coach needs to decide whether they want to go down the path of developing the whole person, or simply confine themselves to athletic or career development. I don't think there's any middle ground.

If the coach chooses the whole person approach they will need to accept that huge sacrifices will be made to their own family and personal life and that there will be influences on their athletes or teams that are beyond their control. The greatest reward to the coach is to witness the personal development of each individual, as well as the performance results. It is an incredibly satisfying and uplifting experience to watch young people grow and know that you have played some small part in their development as a person.

Coaching is about helping a person to develop and grow as an individual first, and as an athlete second.

2. Limitations, yes. Limits, no!

I think it is extremely important to understand the difference between the words 'limitations' and 'limits', as this has a very real impact on the way we think and lead our lives, and therefore the way we influence the lives of others.

Walt Disney was once quoted as saying:

Somehow I can't believe that there are any heights that can't be scaled by a man who knows the secrets of making dreams come true. This special secret, it seems to me, can be summarised in the four C's – curiosity, confidence, courage, constancy, and the greatest of all is confidence. When you believe in a thing, believe in it all the way, implicitly and unquestionably.

All of us have limitations — limitations in our ability to do a job, limitations in our ability to meet someone new, limitations to perform athletically, to sing, to paint or to act. Beyond these sorts of situations or endeavours we may also have limitations simply due to our age, gender, disabilities, financial means, geographic location, ethnicity, left-handedness or right-handedness.

Some of these are a given; we are unable to change them. Some can be changed, but it could take a fair bit of time and effort. However, whatever the limitations may be, accept them for what they are and then set about not limiting oneself to what can be achieved. I look at it this way: I have limitations, yes, but given these, and accepting I can alter some and not others, then there are no limits to what I can achieve.

As we grow from childhood to the lofty world of adulthood, and all the responsibilities that come with this important position in society, we lose the child in us. We lose the ability, the time or even the sense to… dream.

Hence, when we sit down to map out our lives — set a direction, define our goals, work out what is possible and what is not, consider the risks, see what others are doing and what we'd like to do, but then find reasons why we can't do them — we are the only ones setting limits on what we can do, no one else.

Glenn McGrath is famous for his perennial quote at the beginning every new Ashes series when he's asked how the team will perform: 'We will win 5–0.' Glenn has never been one to let limitations of any description dictate to him what limits are achievable.

Acknowledge your limitations, but then realise that the only limits to performance are set by yourself.

3. Remote control

What do Sooty, Mr Squiggle, Punch and Judy, and Bert and Ernie all have in common? They all had great coaches.

Coaching is all about having others say what you would have said yourself. Coaching is about clearly understanding where you are going, or at least where you want to be in a certain time-frame, passionately believing in it, and then working out the means of getting there.

One of the most powerful means of chasing down the coach's vision is for the players, especially the senior players, to become strident advocates for that vision. This process requires:

- Finding the best ways and means to sell a concept, an idea or an innovation to the team leaders. This can be done by one-on-one meetings using information sheets for sharing detail, or encouraging group think-tanks which include an informal agenda, visual demonstrations and a vision of what the end result could be.

- All staff who have the opportunity to influence players being in tune with team direction and having a full understanding of why it is important.

- The provision for regular formal and informal feedback regarding progress.

- When resistance is encountered, which will always occur, weigh up the impact of successful implementation against the need to address the issue immediately. If you choose to delay implementation, careful selection of alternative strategies and a schedule for re-introduction is imperative.

- Chasing the dream, the concept, the idea, the innovation is a continual work in progress, and control of it finding its way into the team system cannot be left to anyone but the coach.

For Australia to be the first international cricket team to score 400 runs in a One-Day International is an example of the process above. I always believed that it could be achieved and I wanted this team to be first. The senior players took some convincing, and even then there were plenty of doubters because it appeared the goal was beyond any team. However, regular conversations with our strike batters, Ricky Ponting, Adam Gilchrist, Matthew Hayden, Andrew Symonds and Mike Hussey, generally in one-on-one or small group meetings, kept the idea and the way of achieving it alive and fermenting.

These methods revolved around better running between wickets, stronger top four partnerships, and additional shot making or ensuring a batter's shots repertoire could be utilised all the time.

We based the vision on the following information: that when the Australian team scored 330-plus runs it was scoring off just over 50 per cent of the balls it received. What were we doing with the other 50 per cent? So this detail was broken down to show what could be achieved by scoring off 60–65 per cent of the available balls.

Again, I was careful how, when and how often this information was presented.

Then it was important that key support staff, such as the specialist coaches, were all on the same page. Our batting coaches Dene Hills and Jamie Siddons would work with each of the batsmen; our analysis coach Richard McInnes would work with all the players and provide them with visual and statistical information that would not conflict with where we were wanting to go; and our fielding coach Mike Young, who could see the potential, would always excite players with the dream.

So, through this process the players became engaged with the concept. Rather than myself or the specialist coaches constantly feeding the idea and the methodologies into our preparations, the players took control in their own way — they owned it!

Good coaching is about guiding the players to a position where they say the same words the coach would say, but without any prompting from the coach.

4. Flags and handbrakes

I cannot lay claim to the words *flags* and *handbreaks*. Dr Phil Jauncey coined these terms. Phil is a sports psychologist who I have had the pleasure of being associated with since I first employed him at the Queensland Bulls in the late 90s.

Take my theory that the principle role of the coach is to become redundant and the only way for this to happen is for the player to become his or her own best coach — that is, they know exactly what is personally required technically, physically, mentally and tactically to give themselves the best chance of performing optimally.

These benchmarks are the individual 'flags' that a player must check off or revert to for preparation and competition. The same can be said about the team as well. By meeting all the 'flags' or checkpoints, both the team and the individual will make good quality decisions consistently and hence performance will be sustainable.

The flip side to 'flags' are the obstacles that prevent good performance — 'handbrakes'. But, as Dr Phil would say, 'If we can't see it and can't measure it, then we can't fix it.'

When we say it is a communication problem or an attitude problem, or the players do not work hard enough, these words are far too broad and open to too many meanings and too much interpretation. To establish the real handbrakes, it is essential that problems are broken down into the actions, the specifics of what is actually happening. It is these specifically identified actions which can then be addressed and rectified.

Transpose generalities into specifics for 'handbrakes' so that they can be resolved effectively. Identify the specific 'flags' of quality performance so that can be repeated consistently.

5. Keeping professionals motivated

There are two important considerations about motivation and motivated athletes. Firstly, the athlete themselves and secondly, the environment in which they operate.

As every person knows, the desire to do something or not comes from within. The external factors and the end reward or punishment matter little. Unless the individual desperately and definitely wants something, then no amount of persuasion will enable them to reach their goals. Even if they did achieve their goals from persuasion, it will only have temporary benefit as they will not be able to fool themselves or those around them for a sustained period.

I never saw myself as a motivator. In the Australian Cricket Team, if a player was not motivated to perform to the high standards set by the team, one of two things were occurring. The coach had provided the athlete with the appropriate environment to enhance his skills and performances, yet the individual was still not motivated to perform. In this case the player would be dropped from the team and the personal reasons found for his lack of motivation.

Or even though the player was motivated to perform, the environment established by the coach was the key de-motivating factor. In this case, the coach needed to be replaced, and be given an opportunity away from the group to address the personal issues that have prevented him from creating the right environment for a sustained performance.

Motivation comes from within and cannot be sustained through external rewards or punishment.

6. How can you coach Test cricketers when you haven't played Test cricket?

These sentiments have been expressed by various people at various times, and definitely pondered by many others. I have never seen myself to be an expert on Test cricket or Test cricketers. What I do bring to the table is expertise in coaching. Coaching among many other things requires an ability to harness the resources that are held within the team. There is an incredible amount of knowledge, experience, innovation and desire residing within the total playing and support staff of the Australian Cricket Team. In addition, there is a range of people outside the team who are able to offer other dimensions and expertise for the benefit of the team.

My approach has always been to provide as much opportunity as possible for this wealth of practical information to be shared by all involved. It is always a disappointment that so-called cricket experts, generally former Test cricketers, like to criticise from a position of ignorance rather than embrace and be embraced by the existing team culture.

Don't be an expert, be credible.

7. Roy's ten-point plan to success

One of the great unknown secrets to the Australian Cricket Team's 2007 World Cup success was a little known meeting between Andrew 'Roy' Symonds and myself as coach. This meeting occurred during the very early stages of the tournament on the island of St Vincent during the final trial game against England.

Roy had been injured during the lead up to the World Cup and was trying to cope with the frustration of not playing and watching his team-mates play. Because of his injury he was not able to do all the things he enjoyed like training, or having a beer.

Beyond boundaries

At the same time he was required to do all the things that were not high on his enjoyment list like rehabilitation, low weight exercises and carefully watching his nutrition. Additionally, Australia had not been performing too well: we had lost our last five ODIs since injury had forced him from the team. There had also been some whinging about our accommodation, training facilities, team organisation, food quality and overall planning for this major event.

From where Roy sat — powerless to do anything on the training paddock or playing field, placed on a close monitoring program, and feeling that there were too many things distracting the team from why they were here, it was time to take action.

He grabbed a pen and paper which, if you knew Roy, showed the gravity of the situation in his mind. For Roy to write anything more than a signature was close to discovering ancient hieroglyphic tablets! Yet, here it was. Having written a ten-point plan, Roy pulled me to one side and proceeded to explain it to me.

And here's Roy's plan, which was one of the keys to us winning the 2007 World Cup:

1. Keep it simple.
2. Know your players.
3. Communication!
4. Show no fear with your decision-making.
5. Lead us.
6. Push those who need to be pushed.

7. Be accountable for everything you do!

8. Yes, you do have to work out of your comfort zone.

9. Jump your final hurdle no matter what!

10. And leave the funnies to others.

I listened, I heard and I hope I delivered on most of his ten-point plan. Roy's words and advice were as good as they were timely.

❑❑❑